BENNETT BOOKS
First Editions

This Bennett Books First Edition has been compiled from previously unpublished material from the literary legacy of J.G. Bennett: a series of six public lectures given by Bennett in London, England, March 8 through April 12, 1954, under the title of "Man's Task and His Reward: A New Conception of Human Destiny Based on the Teaching of G. Gurdjieff." The passage of time has only increased its value.

This book is printed on   acid-free paper.

"The Call"
Tissue paper collage by Edith Wallace.

Author and Art Therapist, Edith Wallace, 85, was a student of Carl Gustav Jung and J.G. Bennett. A practicing Jungian Psychoanalyst in Santa Fe, New Mexico, Dr. Wallace's work is a bridge between the spiritual and psychological worlds. In classes, workshops and private practice, she offers students and clients the living fruits of a long life dedicated to the study of human transformation.

Honored to have Dr. Wallace's collage and cover design "introduce" the material in this book, Bennett Books relates the following story told by Dr. Wallace:

"I am happy to offer this collage, because Mr. Bennett was always very interested in my paintings. Once he accepted some watercolor paintings of mine because they "touched on a problem" of his. After his death, I told his wife Elizabeth Bennett of this incident. Her response: 'That man could learn from *anything!*'"

Making a Soul

Making a Soul

Human Destiny and the
Debt of Our Existence

J.G. Bennett

BENNETT BOOKS

Santa Fe, New Mexico

First Edition
Previously unpublished material. Developed from a series of six public lectures given in London, England by the author under the title of "Man's Task and His Reward: A New Conception of Human Destiny Based on the Teaching of G. Gurdjieff," March 8 through April 12, 1954.

Bennett Books
P.O. Box 1553
Santa Fe, New Mexico 87504

Book and Cover Design: AM Services

Cover Art: Edith Wallace, M.D., Ph.D. "The Call," tissue paper collage. Originally reproduced in her book, *A Queen's Quest: Pilgrimage for Individuation.* (Santa Fe, New Mexico: Moon Bear Press, 1990.) Used here with permission of the artist and Moon Bear Press.

Dedication page photo by Avis Rappoport Licht © 1994 by the photographer.

Library of Congress Cataloging-in-Publication Data
Bennett, John G. (John Godolphin), 1897-1974.
    Making a soul : human destiny and the debt of our existence /
J.G. Bennett. -- 1st ed.
        p.   cm.
    Previously unpublished material developed from lectures given in
1954.
        Includes index.
        ISBN 1-881408-00-0 (pbk. : alk. paper)
        1. Life. 2. Soul 3. Man I. Title.
    BP610.B46147   1995
    128--dc20   94-38285
                                                                CIP

Contents

JOHN G. BENNETT, 1974, THE YEAR OF HIS DEATH

Editor's Note

Over the years following Gurdjieff's death and until his own death, J.G. Bennett periodically gave public talks about Gurdjieff's work. Compare these lectures (1954) with the 1949 lectures that comprise Bennett's book, *Is There Life on Earth?* and you see that the lectures that make up this book already show signs of Bennett coming to his own formulation.

The 1949 talks were very straight down-the-line Gurdjieff. By 1954 this was already beginning to change, and Mr. Bennett was beginning to tell the story in his own words.

"The master said there is one thing in this world which must never be forgotten. If you were to forget everything else, but were not to forget this, there would be no cause to worry, while if you remembered, performed and attended to everything else, but forgot that one thing, you would in fact have done nothing whatsoever. It is as if a king had sent you to a country to carry out one special, specific task. You go to the country and you perform a hundred other tasks, but if you have not performed the tasks you were sent for, it is as if you have performed nothing at all. So man has come into the world for a particular task, and that is his purpose. If he doesn't perform it, he will have done nothing."

—Jeláluddin Rumi, *Table Talk*

"There is in our life a certain very great purpose and we must all serve this Great Common Purpose—in this lies the whole sense and predestination of our life."
—G. Gurdjieff, *All and Everything*

Chapter 1

The Reason for Man's Existence on the Earth

Lecture 1: March 8, 1954

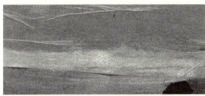

LET US BEGIN by asking ourselves the reason why we are meeting here tonight. To such a question there can be a general answer for us all and a private answer for each one of us. In general, I suppose that you want to learn something that you feel may be important for you or, if not important, at least interesting. The urge to do something comes from a need to be satisfied. If we persevere with these lectures, we may hope that at the end of the course* we shall have moved from where we are today; a relationship will have been established between us; something will have been shared. Not only will you understand better what I have to say but I also will understand it better as a result of my effort to share my knowledge with you. Thus, we can call the general reason for our meeting the urge—that to a greater or lesser degree we all feel—to acquire and to share some new knowledge.

The private reason for our coming together may, on the face of it, be very different for each one of us. Some of you may have realized that it is not enough to wish to live and to act rightly but that one must also know how, and have the power to do it, and you may have seen rather clearly that you neither know how to live nor cannot even do the little that you know. Those of you who have come with such a motive are looking for a practical method, and will judge what I say in terms of its application to your own life problems. At the other extreme, some of you may have been induced by a friend unwillingly to come and hear lectures, supposedly for your own good, and you might be inclined to answer the question "Why are we meeting here?" with "I wish I knew myself." Whether it is from a genuine need or just curiosity or even by mere chance that you have come here, the fact still remains that we, all of us, do have a deep question, and that is: *"Are we making of our lives what we should be making?"* This applies both to our outer life—that is, what we do—and to our inner world—that is, what we *are*.

It would make a great difference to the success of our common undertaking if we could succeed in remembering that we all of us do have this deep question

---

*The chapters in this book have been compiled from transcripts of lectures given as a course of practical study and experiential work based on the ideas and teachings of G.I. Gurdjieff.

and that therefore there is a common need in which we all share. You and I and all normal people must be dissatisfied with the way we live—but we do not sufficiently see that this dissatisfaction that we all share should be the strongest motive for seeking one another out in order to find help. I say this because there are various ways in which a lecturer and his audience can be connected. It is possible for the lecturer to take on himself the active role, to seek to arouse the interest or the feelings of his audience while they sit back passively and simply react to what he may say or do. This relationship of follow-my-leader between an active *one* and a passive *many* is very common in our human life, and, if we reflect upon it, we can see that it is one of the principal reasons why so many things go wrong with us. Another possibility would be for me to refuse to be active and leave it entirely to you to take the initiative, offering to answer your questions but doing so only insofar as you, with activity and persistence, were to press me to tell you what I know, and to share what I understand. That kind of relationship would be very good for realizing our common aim, for you, through making an effort, would earn whatever you might receive, and every sensible person knows that what we do not earn can never be ours.

We are, however, unaccustomed to what can be called a centripetal initiative—that is, an initiative directed from the circumference toward the center—and we cannot hope to start with such a relationship. Nevertheless, I want you to understand that if our task is to be accomplished, success depends at least as much upon you as it does upon me. What is it that I wish you to bring? Subjects upon which I shall speak do not presuppose for their study a scientific training and wide experience of life, much knowledge of history or philosophy, or deep religious convictions—although, of course, all these things are very valuable if we know how to use them. All that I ask of you is to bring a readiness to make a genuine effort to think for yourselves, putting aside all your preconceived ideas, even what you believe you have already learned in reading about Gurdjieff's Teaching. I want you to reach your own conclusion and form your own convictions about the task that lies before men and women as we live here on the earth.

Let us start by examining the title of tonight's lecture. It is "The Reason for Man's Existence on the Earth."

What do we mean by "reason"? You will notice that I put to you the question, "What is the reason for our meeting tonight?" and if you examine the answer you will see that it draws your attention to a connection between something that occurred inside you and something that has happened outside you. The first was your own response to the idea of hearing something about Gurdjieff's Teaching; the second is your presence with a lot of other people in this hall tonight. I want you also to notice the difference between a reason and a cause. Your reason for coming is quite different from the cause of your coming. This may have been an advertisement you saw in the paper or something you were told by a friend, but many people saw the advertisements or were told about these lectures and did not come. What is the difference? All were subjected to the action of the same cause, but not all had a reason for coming. A reason is also different from a purpose. A purpose is something in the future, and it generally means something I can picture to myself and formulate as an aim. A reason is something more direct than a cause or a purpose, and, whether profound or trivial, it always comes from a need. That is why reasons are important and why I took for the title "The Reason for Man's Existence on the Earth" in order to open with you the question whether or not man is needed for something. If so, that need—and its fulfillment—is the reason for his existence. If, on the contrary, man is not needed for anything, then we should be bound to say that there is no reason for his existence. I want you to remember this and think about it carefully because it may not be obvious and yet the answer matters very much. Moreover, it must be your own answer, not borrowed from someone else.

In order to clarify the question, let us ask it about something simpler and humbler than man; for example, the grass of the field and the trees of the forest. Is there some reason why they exist on the earth? We could answer from our knowledge of biology that without green vegetation there could be no animals and no men living on the earth. All our food comes from green vegetation, which supports our life by its ableness to transform energy coming from the sun. Animals and men need food, and the existence of vegetation enables this need to be satisfied. We can therefore say that men and animals provide a reason for the existence of vegetation, but I would like you to notice that I have not said either that green vegetation is the cause of man's existence or that it is there for the purpose of serving man. We want to get rid of the words "cause" and "purpose," which are misleading, and keep fast to the words "reason" and "need," which refer to something that we actually experience.

The more closely we look at life around us, the more do we find evidence that a relationship of need does connect one form of life with another. Not only this, but living creatures also are connected by a relationship of need with the energy that reaches us in the light and warmth of the sun, with the chemical substances of the earth's surface, with the water, and with the air. From such considerations we can reach the very important conclusion that in order to be what it is, to live its own life, everything is in need of some support and, moreover, that this support usually comes from a lower level of existence. This is illustrated by the need that plants have for minerals and animals have for plants.

If we look at our own human life, we can see how many things we need, and we might be inclined to say that everything exists as it does in order to satisfy man's needs and that therefore man is the reason for the existence of animals, plants, minerals, sun, moon, and stars. Now this is exactly what men have said and believed in the past and what many say and believe today. Not only have people said and believed this, but nearly all human activity is based on the assumption that everything exists just to supply man's needs and that he is entitled to make use of everything as he finds it, just as suits him best. There is nothing, from an atom to a star, that man would not be prepared to destroy if he thought it would make his life more comfortable or safer. This is a fact, but I think that we cannot feel altogether happy about it and must suspect that there is a catch somewhere.

It is rather strange that even people who are disturbed by man's destructiveness do not go on and ask the further question: What about man himself? May he not also exist to serve a need? May there not be the same kind of reason for his existence as there is for that of animals, plants, minerals, and the energy of the sun and the stars, or is he somehow different, standing outside the economy of the universe, a law unto himself? In the past, people have answered this question with an unhesitating "yes." Man is different, they have said, and he does not exist to serve needs of the same kind as the living creatures and inanimate matter that surround him. This belief in the uniqueness of man is common to believers and unbelievers, to theists and materialists. The former believe that man was created by God, and is responsible only to God. The latter hold that he arose by some kind of accident and can thus be responsible only to himself. On either view it would be inaccurate to speak of a reason for man's existence. Accident can have no need, and God, as he is generally understood by religious people, is also supposed to be infinite and almighty, outside the universe and needing nothing from any part of it, including man. Religious people have thought, like [the English poet] John Milton, that God does not need either man's work or his own gifts: "Who best bear his mild yoke, they serve him best."

I want you to understand that either way of looking at our human situation is altogether wrong. Both disregard the question of the need, and therefore of the reason, for man's existence. Because of this, they have led to disastrous misunderstandings, for both views destroy in man any sense of responsibility, for if we are not needed and there is no reason for our existence, we cannot rightly be called responsible.

Let us spend a few minutes to see what science can tell us about our problem. Modern science has done much to make man's life materially comfortable, but, on the whole, it has confused him about the fundamental questions. Nevertheless, it should have taught us at least one thing; namely, that we men do not occupy a privileged position in the universe. There are great realms of existence that stand completely outside our experience. Physical and chemical sciences have opened our eyes to a world of very small things that we can never enter, and astronomy and astrophysics have shown us the immensity of the universe—an immensity into which it is inconceivable that man should ever penetrate. This should be humbling to our feeling of self-importance, but there is worse to come. Biology teaches us that our human experience is closely tied up with the processes of the body, that we can only think and feel and know and do what our body allows us to do and when and in the manner that our body allows. Our character is not the expression of our own will but the result of the chemistry of our blood. A change of chemistry will completely transform both our experience and our behavior. Moreover, we must also learn from science that the beliefs about God that men have held in the past have been little more than tribal superstitions. The universe has existed and was full of significance long before there were men to entertain notions of divinity. Everything is on a far vaster scale than our grandfathers could realize, and their speculations about God and the universe seem to us today like childish nonsense.

Must we on this account suppose that man exists by accident in an alien world that does not know of his presence and does not need him? Until recently, this was the view held by the majority of scientists, but something in us revolts and asserts very decisively that it cannot be true. Something tells us, stronger than logic and more reliable than feeling, that we are responsible for something and therefore that we are needed—and that whether we wish it or not, the reason for our existence must be fulfilled. Even if we want to shirk responsibility, we find some deep voice saying in us that it will not do and that there is a task that we cannot betray. This is remarkable, considering that, for the most part, the life of man proceeds as if he were responsible toward nothing but himself or toward the society to which he happens to belong or, at most, toward the whole human race. Irresponsibility is very comfortable, and it corresponds to our natural impulse to satisfy only the needs of which we feel the immediate urge and not to trouble ourselves with responsibilities that may be higher and more important but that do not touch us directly. If then there is something in us that cannot take this easy, comfortable way, this is strong evidence that there is a reality we usually disregard and that this reality has something to do with the reason for our existence on the earth.

So far, we have not reached anything definite or convincing. On the one hand, we can see that without a reason there is no foundation on which to construct a plan of life. The argument is objective but perhaps too remote to be convincing as applied to ourselves. On the other hand, we have our own deep feeling of responsibility that tells us that we are needed for something. It is a subjective conviction and perhaps too intimate to be applied to the whole human problem.

There is, however, a third argument that links the two together, one that we cannot help accepting when once we understand it. This is that if there is a reason for anything, there must be a reason for everything. It is quite impossible to imagine a little oasis that makes sense in a vast endless desert of nonsense. It is impossible to imagine that there are small needs unless there are also big needs and that there are little reasons unless there are also great reasons. Now there is no doubt that, on the scale of our own experience, needs and responsibilities are real and, moreover, that they are not confined just to our human life. Between a cat and a kitten there is a relationship of need and responsibility, and we are saying something true and significant when we say that the needs of her kittens are the reason for the mother cat's behavior. This does not mean that the cat recognizes and understands the need or acts with a conscious purpose but simply that in an obvious sense we can and must speak of there being a reason for what she does.

I think you will understand what I mean if I say that "reason is indivisible." If there are reasons anywhere, then there must be reasons everywhere, and hence also a reason why we men exist on the earth. It may seem to you that I have made heavy weather of something that you would have accepted without question, but you must not forget that nothing whatever in the life of man proceeds as if there were a reason for his existence, outside of his own impulses and

needs. People either do not ask themselves the reason for their existence or else
they accept some ready-made answer without even stopping to ask themselves
what it means. We men are really very stupid. We either will not look beyond
our noses or else we will insist upon staring beyond the stars. We think only in
terms of this visible life and its comforts and discomforts or else we think of a
God, a Creator, who is infinite, above all needs. We may think of God as a stern
ruler, making demands that we have to fulfill, or as a loving father, caring for our
eternal, no less than our temporal, welfare. But on either view we do not think of
need; therefore, we do not look for the reason of our existence. I will go further
and say that because we do not face and resolve this one question, all human life
is sick and that we do no more, at best, than palliate some of the symptoms of
the sickness. Perhaps you will understand now why I have taken you through all
these arguments, which may have seemed rather more suited to some abstract
philosophical discussion than to a meeting of people from all walks of life who
have come together in search of a practical answer to their own deep questions.
The truth is that we cannot even begin to think rightly about our deep problems
unless we have some idea of the reason for our existence on the earth.

Let us now address ourselves to Gurdjieff's answer to the question, "Why
does man exist on the earth?" First of all, it must surely be obvious that we do
not exist just to satisfy our own impulses. A reason cannot be self-centered;
therefore, if really nothing in the world matters except ourselves, there is no reason why we should do anything. All talk about "the greatest good of the greatest
number" is nonsense, both in philosophy and in practice. If the reason for our
existence is not derived from something greater than ourselves, then it is no reason at all and irresponsibility is the only law. But even animals are not irresponsible. I would go further and say that animals are more responsible than men, for
we can see that whereas man thinks and works only for himself, animals and
even plants serve needs greater than their own existence. In this observation lies
the key to answering our question. The interconnectedness of living and nonliv-
ing existence all around us must convince us that everything that exists provides
something necessary for the existence of something else.

Let us assume for a moment that this holds good for man also; that is, that
man by his existence provides something that is needed by some being higher
than himself—as, for example, grass provides something that is needed for the
life of sheep and cows, or manure provides something necessary for the life of
plants. We must then ask ourselves what could be man's contribution toward the
needs of a form of life higher than his own? In asking this question, we have
already come a long way because I suppose that many of you do realize that this
is really the most important question for man, upon the answer to which the
whole understanding of our destiny depends. So that we can be quite clear what
the question is, let us consider one or two illustrations. Man with his hairless
body needs clothing, and wool is one of the chief materials out of which clothes
are made. A sheep, in providing wool, gives man something that he needs, and
because he needs this, a man looks after his sheep, taking care that they are fed
and kept healthy. The sheep that give the best wool are highly valued and cho-

sen for breeding, whereas a strain of sheep that gives poor wool is worth keeping only for mutton; that is, to give food. Thus, a sheep supplies man's needs in two ways, one of which involves its own death, whereas the other does not. Another example can be seen in the grains of wheat, which also serve man's needs in two ways. One is to be ground into flour, baked into bread, and eaten. The other is to be planted in the ground, where the grain, it is true, dies but is born again as a new wheat plant, and so its life is transmitted to another generation. I have chosen these illustrations to suggest to you that there are quite different ways in which a given form of life can serve another, but both the ways are deeply significant. They go to the very root of the existence and the life of that which gives and of that which receives.

If man exists for a reason, then this reason must certainly be as definite and as significant as those for which grass and grain, sheep and cattle exist on the earth. I want you to notice that we have already begun to learn something about the relationships of need. First of all, we can see that there is a scale of existence between the members of which there is the relationship of mutual need. Water, air, and minerals supply the needs of green vegetation, which in turn gives food for animal life. Plants and animals give food for man, but man cannot feed directly upon minerals or convert air and sunshine into food, like vegetables can. If there is too big a gap between one level of existence and another, there cannot be a direct relationship of mutual need. If you could fully grasp all the significance of the facts that man cannot feed directly upon minerals and that he cannot transform air and sunshine into food like the grass can, then you would have discovered one of the keys to understanding the reason why everything, including man, exists as it does.

The second important point to be noted is that wherever we look at reasons and needs, we discover death and rebirth. We should therefore expect that death and birth have also some intimate connection with the reason for our own existence. This may remind us that the most ancient beliefs about man and his destiny—beliefs that have entered into all conceptions of religion everywhere—have connected the life of man with the mystery of the grain that dies in order to produce a harvest.

Having taken these illustrations about as far as we can safely go, let us make a fresh start by examining human life as we know it and asking what there is in man's existence that could serve the needs of a higher being. The most obvious thing about a man is his body. Our own bodies make the first and greatest demands upon our energy and our time. The greater part of the existence of the average man is spent in working to provide food, shelter, and clothing for himself and his family and in resting and sleeping to enable his body to restore its energies. Our bodies are important to us, but we can scarcely look upon them as the reason for our existence. However much care we may bestow upon it, there is only one end to our body, and that is death. In order to keep it going sixty, seventy, eighty years, we have devoted all that time and trouble, and the end of it all is a corpse rotting on the charnel ground. What could be more absurd than to suppose that the reason for our existence is to produce a rotting corpse?

Apart from the immediate needs of their own bodies, ordinary men and women spend much of their time and energy in producing and rearing children. Could we then say that the reason for our existence is the continuation of our own race? To this the same argument applies as before, with the only difference that we work to make a line of corpses on a belt conveyor instead of one at a time. Whether it is my own body or my children's bodies or those of my children's children to the remotest posterity, the end is always the same. On the highest estimation, dead bodies serve as food for worms or as manure for the soil, and to regard this end as the reason for our existence would be to reverse the whole chain of reasons that we found in the ascent of existence from mineral matter to man. If it were true, then all existence would be a cycle returning endlessly and uselessly into itself, and the word "reason" would be a mockery.

If we are to look beyond man's body for a reason for his existence, the obvious direction in which to search is toward his *works*. Man differs from the animals primarily because he is a maker—*Homo faber*. Here again, we must admit that a great part of what man makes is concerned only with the preservation of his own existence. He plows the fields and waters them, gathers food and cooks it. He builds houses and furnishes them. He makes himself clothes and wears them. In all these activities he is only serving the body that perishes. A greater part of all that man makes is directed in this way to the necessities of his bodily existence or, at most, to his physical comfort and relaxation. If we look at the remainder we discover—and the discovery should amaze us—that a considerable part of man's energies is devoted to making things that destroy the body he takes such pains to preserve. I refer not only to the weapons of war but to harmful amusements and dangerous habits. These productions that either destroy the body or maim it or riddle it with disease absorb so much of man's energy that we can safely say that 90 percent of all his activities are concerned either with preserving his body or with destroying it—or at least shortening the term of its existence.

Since we can scarcely argue that the reason for man's life is to find means of destroying himself, we must look at the remaining 10 percent if we are to have much hope of finding an answer to our problem. This relatively small residue of activity is directed chiefly toward the satisfaction of what can be called man's spiritual needs. There is a force acting in man that makes him curious, hungry for impressions. Ideally, this hunger should be satisfied in the enjoyment of truth and beauty; that is, the search for real knowledge, the contemplation of nature and works of art, and also in actions performed for the welfare of others. We know well how in our modern life these noble impulses are debased and how in their place we feed upon a morbid curiosity about the misfortunes of others, of which our newspapers are full, and upon the spurious excitements of sport and entertainment. When these are put aside, there remains of all human activity only a very tiny residue of achievements that can be regarded as having some intrinsic or permanent value outside the bodily wants and the egoistic fears and weaknesses of man himself. The construction of fine buildings, the creation of works of art, scientific discovery, and the philosopher's search for truth are names that disguise much triviality and self-seeking, but there is certainly a remainder, a residue that has a value beyond mere self-preservation or self-destruction or the satisfaction of egoism.

Where are these great works of man? For thousands of years—before the dawn of history—man has had the impulse to create beautiful works and to discover the truth. There is no doubt at all that these impulses were stronger in the remote past than they are today. The cities of ancient Greece and of Egypt, India, Babylon, and Sumeria, devoted a far greater part of their total activity to the creation of beauty and the search for truth than any modern city does today. What has remained of these achievements? Nothing but mounds of dust, crumbling ruins, and perhaps a few marvelous works of art carried off to lose their significance in the incongruous environment of a museum. Last year [in 1953] I made a journey through many of the most ancient cities of the world and saw the ruins of Babylon and of Nineveh and of Ur and the cities of the Flood, and nothing struck me more forcibly than the contrast between the great achievements of those ancient peoples and the utter destruction of their works. Not only man himself but also his works perish. A work of art, that for thousands of years arouses an experience of beauty, is a great achievement, but when it vanishes nothing remains. Even the mightiest city in its ruins serves no other purpose than to remind us of our own mortality and the perishableness of everything that is human.

We have exhausted the catalog of all that is visible in the life of man. Not finding the reason for man's existence in what he does, perhaps we can discover it in *what he is,* his inner world and its contents. When we ask ourselves what man *is,* we meet at once a familiar answer to the question as to the reason for his existence; namely, that he exists not for the sake of his body but for the sake of his soul. It even seems plausible to say that the reason for man's existence is the purification or perfecting of the soul; but this implies that man has a soul and, moreover, a soul that can exist apart from the body, for if it perished with the body, it would be open to the same objections as before. Unfortunately, the soul, when we look for it, proves to be elusive, if not illusory. All the properties that formerly were attributed to the soul are now seen to be consequences of the construction of the nervous system and the chemistry of the blood. These are the things that make man be what he is, behave as he does, reacting automatically to the action of his environment upon his organs of sense. Physiology and psychology have demonstrated beyond the possibility of doubt that man as we know him is a complicated chemical and electrical mechanism, producing automatic reactions according to his hereditary predisposition and the results of his early training and the experiences of life. The more we know about what man is and how he works, the less justification do we find for supposing that there is present in him anything like the soul in which people used to believe.

This is not really a new discovery, for 2,500 years ago, Gautama Buddha and other Indian thinkers, such as Makkali Gosala, produced just the same arguments to demolish the then current belief that there is in man an independent, animating principle—the *atman* or breath—that is the same as what we call the *anima* or the soul. Putting it shortly, we can say that no evidence can be found, either in the inner life or the outer behavior of man, that justifies a belief that he has a soul. This may seem very strange to you since it is commonly supposed that anyone who believes in God must also believe in the soul, and, as I am certainly not an atheist, you might expect me to be an animist; that is, one who believes in the soul. The two beliefs are quite independent, both historically and psychologically, and I would ask you further to notice that although many people pay lip service to belief in the soul, no one takes this belief seriously, for, if they did, they would scarcely devote 90 percent or more of their energies to the body that perishes and concern themselves so little with the needs of the supposed immortal soul. The truth is that man does not and cannot believe in the soul because he has not got one, and, at bottom, he knows only too well that he has not.

Moreover, if there were in all of us a ready-made soul, assured of immortality, then the soul itself could hardly be the reason for our existence. If our souls were wanted for some higher purpose, then this present life could have been dispensed with and the soul could have been taken in all its newborn purity to serve the purpose for which it was intended. We must observe here a very important aspect of our problem; namely, that the reasons are not connected with what things are but with what they are able to give. The reason we keep sheep is not that they are sheep but that they can give wool. The grass transforms air, water, and sunshine into food, the cow transforms grass into milk, and if there is a reason for man's existence then it must be also in some kind of transformation.

Now if we ask ourselves what it is that is constantly being transformed in man himself, we can see at once that it is his *experience,* his sense perceptions, his thoughts, his feelings, his joys, his sorrows, his strivings, his moments of enlightenment, and his moments of love. At first, it might seem that these are even more perishable than a body and pass away into nothingness as soon as they have arisen. There is a great mistake here, for all these have the quality of energy, and energy does not perish—only its visible forms and outer manifestations change. Bodies die, works perish, but energy remains, undergoing endless transformations, rising and falling in the scale of existence but never destroyed. Since our human experiences are also a form of energy, they cannot be destroyed but must go somewhere, and here at last we begin to find the answer to the question we have been pursuing. Out of every life is the possibility of something that serves the need of another life, and out of human life also there is the possibility of energy needed for a higher level of existence. This is the reason for man's existence on the earth. All existence is energy, and all energy is needed for something; but the energy of human experience is of a different quality and a different significance from the experiences that can arise in animals and vegetables, in minerals, in water, or in air.

Science teaches us that everything is energy, but not all energy can be used in the same way. The heat energy in boiling water will cook an egg but it will not melt iron. The energy in an arc lamp will melt iron but cannot think. The energy of the nervous system of man can think but it cannot make a child, or add one cubit to his stature. Every need requires some form of energy for its satisfaction, but energy must be of the right quality and intensity. This is the secret of the relationships that we found earlier between minerals and plants, plants and animals, animals and man. We can therefore say with complete confidence that the reason for man's existence must be to produce energy of a particular intensity and quality. Human experience obviously differs very much in the quality of energy it produces. Much of it is to all intents and purposes the same as that of animals. When a man eats or lies down to sleep or mates, his experiences can differ very little from those of any other animal's. The forms of experience that are characteristically human are those that go beyond the needs and impulses of the body, beyond even the satisfactions of human intercourse, though these also cannot differ very much from the social impulses of animals. That which is truly human is the capacity for joy and suffering, for hope and fear, that leads him beyond himself, and we must, if we are to find the reason for human existence, look for it in these experiences and here alone.

When we study these impulses closely, we find that they are intimately connected with the experiences of death and birth; joy and suffering are *the meeting point of yes and no;* and "yes" and "no" are themselves the impulses of birth and death. If we look still more closely, we can see that man is never really touched by anything but these two impulses. Where death and birth are absent, experience is empty, life is a process without meaning, coming from nowhere and going nowhere, and in this process man himself, man as he is, disappears into the machine.

Nothing distinguishes one man from another more than the way in which they respond to the impulses of death and birth. In these lectures, I shall try to help you to see why this is so and how through understanding these things we can put our own lives in order. For the present, I wish only to restate the answer to our question in a form that I think you will now not find difficult to understand: *Man exists on the earth in order to produce energy of a certain intensity and quality, and this energy is liberated through his experiences of joy and suffering and through his response to the forces of death and birth.* The energy produced in this way is required for a form of life higher than man himself, just as man in his turn requires energies produced by forms of life lower than his own. Everything in the universe is maintained through the transformations of energy, and it is to these transformations that Gurdjieff refers in the quote with which I began this lecture: "There is in our life a certain very great purpose and we must all serve this Great Common Purpose—in this lies the whole sense and predestination of our life."

We are now left with the last and strangest question of all. What being or beings greater than ourselves require the energy that is released by our human experiencing? If we could know the answer to this question, we should have discovered the reason for our existence. The question is only strange because it is utterly foreign to us to suppose that we men could stand in relation to some higher being in the same position as our sheep and cows stand toward us, and yet we have to admit that there is nothing scientifically or logically absurd, or even improbable, in such a notion. It agrees with the fundamental principle of all science, which is the continuity and self-consistency of the natural order. On the contrary, it would be absurd to suppose that whereas all nature is connected through the transformations of energy, man alone should somehow stand outside this universal law.

We should not be surprised that we cannot see for ourselves how and for what we are needed. Sheep do not understand the reason for their existence. At most, they may observe that from time to time their wool is sheared. Perhaps they may even realize that they are slaughtered before the natural term of their life has ended. Do you suppose that nothing like that happens to us men? Are we not also from time to time subjected to painful experiences that deprive us of our wool—that is, our comfortable sense of security and well-being—and is it not true that our lives are far shorter than they should be according to our natural constitution? Physiologists tell us that there is no reason why man should not live in full exercise of his faculties for a hundred and fifty or two hundred years. We ought to see for ourselves that we should need a much longer life if we were to have any real hope of understanding our destiny and learning how to direct it. Man grows old and dies just as he is beginning to gain experience of life and to have the possibility of impartial judgment. We ought from such observations to understand that our life does not proceed according to what we want. It is not arranged for our own welfare but appears to be under the control of some power that we do not understand—a power that uses us for its purposes—even when we think that we serve our own egoism. Anyone who is capable of studying human life impartially must reach the conclusion that we exist for some reason other than the satisfaction of our own personal wishes or the welfare of our race.

I want at this point to remind you of an observation we made a little while ago; namely, that when we study the relationships of need in the natural order, we find that each form of life serves the need of another life, higher—but not very much higher—than its own. We should therefore expect that we men also exist to supply the needs of some form of existence, great compared with ourselves but not infinitely great.

Now when we look about us, we can see the forms of life that are far greater than man, both in scale of size and time and also in the complexity and fullness of their existence. These are the heavenly bodies, the stars, the sun, the planets, and the moons. Only a very clumsy, heavy-footed thinking would suppose that the heavenly bodies are nothing more than inert lumps of matter, without consciousness, without experience, and without a reason for their existence. If once we understand that the sun and the stars must be alive—and, moreover, alive with a far greater intensity of experience than we can ever know—then we may well ask ourselves also whether these may not be the beings whose needs furnish the reason for our existence. We can learn much from the study of analogy, and it will be profitable to draw a comparison between the body of man, composed as it is of thousands of millions of living cells, held together by a bony framework, and nourished by the stream of blood that flows through its veins, and the earth, with its thousands of millions of living creatures, held together by its rocky foundations and nourished by the streams of the rivers and the oceans.

Such analogies are to be found everywhere, and when they are closely studied, they convince us that everything in the universe is built upon one common pattern. This is Gurdjieff's doctrine of cosmoses, which helps us to understand how it can be that man—who occupies in relation to the earth a position not unlike that of the brain cells in our own bodies—can, notwithstanding his small size, play a significant part in the energy transformations of the great heavenly bodies.

Before finishing tonight, I must make one last and all-important distinction. This concerns the way in which the reason for man's existence is fulfilled. Our experience becomes charged with a peculiar penetrating energy when it touches the question of death and birth, but at all times we find ourselves subject to various disturbing influences that produce in us responses of joy or sorrow. We are constantly confronted with the choice of "yes" and "no"; and in the way we make this choice, we can change the quality of our own experience. We stand in a different position from other forms, which are properly called lower, just because they lack the power to change by their own decision the quality of their experiences. About this property of man I shall have much to say in the next few lectures. You have probably heard that Gurdjieff taught that man as we know him is asleep, that he lives in a dream world with very few real experiences, and, moreover, that man who is asleep can produce energy of a quality that is only suitable for satisfying the needs of the moon. Such a man is no more than an automatic transformer of energy. Nothing that is in him can be called his own. It is precisely in this sense that I said before that ordinary men and women have no soul. To have a soul is to be oneself, but that is to be master of one's own energies. Man such as we know him is not his own master, and he has no power over his energies. The special property of man that makes him different from any other being of whom we have knowledge is that he can acquire conscious control over his own energies and so bring about a transformation of his own being that can be called the acquisition of a soul. The man in whom this transformation does not take place is and remains a passive apparatus for converting energy, just as grass makes carbohydrates or a sheep makes wool. He serves his purpose, but when it is served he is finished with and he disappears from the scene. If, on the contrary, he exercises the power latent in him of converting energy by his own intentional experiencing, then he can become himself; that is, a conscious, active and effectual participant in the realization of the Great Purpose that we all exist to serve.

So we have come back to our starting point when, I spoke of our meeting tonight and said there was a general reason and a private reason why we should be here. It is the same with our existence on the earth. There is a general or public reason in which we all share—that is, to transform energy by our birth and death and by the experiences of our life. This we must do whether we know it or not. It is an obligation from which there is no escape. The second reason concerns us personally, and it is the possibility latent in each one of us of becoming ourselves, of creating something in us that can truly be called an immortal soul. However this second reason can be fulfilled only after the first has been discharged. It is a privilege that man can earn and not a right that he can demand.

I have said enough for the time being. We have three-quarters of an hour before we need stop, and you can, if you wish, use this time for asking any questions about what I have said.

QUESTIONS AND ANSWERS

Question: When you said that a man could lift himself on to a higher plane, do you mean that a man such as yourself or myself could become the end product of this process that was described? Am I being very naive about this?

J.G.B.: You must understand that man in his automatic state has nothing psychically permanent. All that has any stability in him is his own body, his nervous system, and so on, but his psychic states are quite fluid. It can be said he has no permanent "I." His "I" is always changing. That does not matter so long as he is only being used as an automatic transformer of energy. For that, he can be a hundred different people every minute; but if he wants to be *himself*, he has to be different. That also needs food, a different kind of food from what is needed for the transient bundle of changing experiences that ordinary people are. To be himself ,he has partly to find and partly to make himself, the energy that is able to give him a permanent self. It is a concrete thing that we have to learn, how and where to find that food. You ask whether man can become such a being that he is able to have something in him that does not perish because he is able to eat a different sort of food? He can, but it needs a different kind of food. This does not mean that man ceases to have an obligation to participate in the General Process of energy transformation. That he must always do. We never can escape from our obligation toward that.

Q.: You said that we are food products for a higher being, and as we depend in particular on the lower being for our own food and we place sheep on the earth, do you imply that the higher beings placed us on this earth for the benefit of their consumption?

J.G.B.: The question here is, has man been put upon this earth by some higher beings in order to serve their needs in the way that we use our sheep, and so on? You must understand that we do not create sheep and we do not create wheat. We have, however, ourselves adapted these to our own needs. We have been absolutely ruthless about it. We have killed off a greater part of the animal life of the earth that did not happen to suit our needs, and we have bred in increasing numbers the forms of life we do need. We have destroyed the forests in order to plant what we need. We have not created anything, but we encourage what we think we need and discourage what we think we do not need. It is the same with man. The power that needs man did not create him. His Creator is a being much greater, but we cannot doubt that there is a higher power that uses man. Nothing would make sense if it were not so. That power tends to do just the same sort of thing with us as we do with our domestic animals; that is, see that they live in such a way that they give us what we want. Supposing that one of our sheep were to take it into its head to change its mode of existence altogether! To stop giving wool and not to be killed for mutton. It would have to run away and live in the mountains. This is hard and dangerous, but if it saw its situation, it might decide to do so and take the risk of living without the sort of care that man gives to it. In the same way, if we are prepared to take the risk of going into a dangerous and difficult existence, we may be able to save ourselves from being sheared and save ourselves from going into mutton.

Q.: These higher beings, are they of physical nature, or are they something beyond that?

J.G.B.: Man is both of physical nature and something beyond that. So we should expect higher beings also to have a complex existence, perhaps even more so than ourselves. Man as we know him consists of three parts. He is not only a physical nature, he has in him one part that has the possibility that I spoke of, of becoming an immortal soul. He has also something else in him that is neither the one nor the other but between the two. So man is not just physical. That complexity of organization is necessary for the transformation of energy. If man were only a bodily organism, he could only do certain kinds of things. If he were only a consciousness, he could only do certain other things. It is because he is both that he has such rich potentialities. We should expect the same about beings on a higher level also. If we accept the principle that everything is likely to be made on one single pattern, then, if there are higher beings, we should not expect those higher beings to be monsters. We should expect them to have a rational organization like, but more perfect than, our own.

Q.: Do the sheep expect their higher beings to have a rational organization?

J.G.B.: At each stage, there is a little bit more possibility of understanding the situation. Minerals understand very little about their situation. Plants certainly can understand more. We cannot look at the life of plants without being quite sure that they know something about what they need and where they are going. Animals decidedly more. We men more still; and with us, there is this most important thing—that we have it in us to understand our situation more and more clearly if we choose.

Q.: I think perhaps my question is partly answered by your answer to the last one. If man's purpose is to create energy for the higher beings, have we any means of finding out what the purpose of the higher being is?

J.G.B.: We can at least see that the hierarchy of being goes far beyond this solar system of ours. In my opinion, it cannot be just an accident that these ideas that Gurdjieff began to teach forty or fifty years ago should agree so remarkably well with what science is discovering about the structure and interrelationships of the universe. Gurdjieff taught that reciprocal maintenance—or, as he called it, the Trogoautoegocratic process, by which everything that exists supports the existence of something else—is of universal validity. Almost daily, astronomers are making discoveries that show how complex are the energy relationships of a great structure like the galaxy—how wonderful the coordinated distribution and renewal of energy—and, moreover, we are certainly only at the beginning of our knowledge of all this. If by the working of a great law—which certainly won't be the "law of human wisdom"—we are able to go on living in peace for some time, there is a great chance that man will come to understand a great deal about his situation on the earth simply as a consequence of scientific discovery. Maybe that will begin to have some influence on our lives. It has not had much influence up until now, perhaps even a bad influence, but it may begin to have a good influence.

Q.: Cannot one compare our present existence to the medieval feudal system, which in time gradually became more democratic? Shall we not become more equal to the super being above?

J.G.B.: Why should you suppose that? Do you think that grass will become more like cows, or cows will develop human characteristics? Then they might refuse to be cows any more.

Q.: It is more or less a historical process?

J.G.B.: As far back as we have knowledge—it may be twenty thousand years—of what man has been like, he has always been the same. Man twenty thousand years ago was certainly just as clever as we are and made just as extraordinary, perhaps even more extraordinary, inventions, so there is no historical reason for supposing that man will change in another twenty thousand years, and that is enough time for us to take into account.

Q.: How does Gurdjieff explain the reversal of the process that you have put before us tonight? Do lower organisms consume higher organisms, for example, parasites consume caterpillars? Man's moral order is destroyed through the medium of volcanic eruptions and natural cataclysms of that kind.

J.G.B.: About natural cataclysms. One cannot tell in general, without detailed study, whether in a given case it is the operation of a law of a higher level or just accident because both can occur. I wanted tonight specially to focus our attention on the upward movement of life that goes through everything, but this has to go against some resistance. There cannot be birth without death. There cannot be a movement up without a movement down—just as there cannot be "yes" without "no."

Q.: Is it the purpose of the Teaching to enable us to produce a better food, because the food is of no use to us as it is only of use to the higher beings?

J.G.B.: I purposely continued an extra ten minutes this evening in order to answer that question in advance. I said we have the possibility—while fulfilling the inevitable reason for our existence—also to do something more as well. It is as if there were allotted to us a certain quota of unavoidable experiences of joy and suffering that we have to go through whether we like it or not. If we live passively, that is all that will happen to us. However, if we are ready to accept more than that, to enter more deeply into the process, then not only can we do what is required of us but something more can enter into us to create our own being. I had in mind to keep before you the difference between the general reason for existing, in which everyone shares, and a private reason that each one of us may have *if we choose*. Gurdjieff teaches that there is something man has to do whether he likes it or not, and there is something he can do if he chooses. He has to transform energy whether he likes it or not, but if he chooses, he can become something more.

Q.: Is it not possible or credible, when you think of the life of higher beings, that one life should not be sufficient to assess our use and that we must take reincarnation into account? What have you to say about reincarnation?

J.G.B.: Reincarnation is the reusing of wasted fragments. You know [the Norwegian poet and dramatist] Henrik Ibsen's *Peer Gynt?* He has a very beautiful illustration, which he must have learned from some source of real knowledge, of a button molder whom Peer Gynt meets and who asks him, "Can you show me that you have become yourself?" Peer realizes that he cannot answer this question and runs away because he knows if he cannot answer the question, he must go into the ladle to be remolded to make other buttons. That is what reincarnation is—going into the ladle. We have the possibility of working in such a way as to bring about the transformation that will make us into immortal souls, and only then we can escape from the button molder's ladle.

Q.: Is our Creator interested in whether we acquire an immortal soul or not?

J.G.B.: It is the one thing in which our Creator is interested. The only thing about man in which our Creator is interested is that.

Q.: Is the moon one of these higher beings or is she merely the home of something?

J.G.B.: I am not going to pretend to you that I know the answer to such a question. I have tried to tell you what I have learned from Gurdjieff and the result of my own studies over many years and the conclusions that I have reached. My own personal conviction about this is that the moon is coming to birth, a being not yet born, and therefore needing certain energy for the process of birth.

Q.: Is there any room for free will in your system, and what is your reaction to fear or a nihilistic approach? Fear of death or suicide?

J.G.B.: This question of free will is one of the main themes of an upcoming lecture [*see* chapter 4] and it is much too long to speak about in a few minutes. About that question of repudiating our responsibility, refusing to transform energy for someone else, and removing ourselves from the scene—it certainly does not work. Man cannot escape from his obligation that way. When I say that man has no soul, I do not mean that man has nothing that may for a time survive death and that has to pay for the consequences of his life. That is something quite different. There is something in man that reaps the rewards and pays for the consequences of his life, but it is not an immortal soul. It is an intermediate formation that is not permanent. That is different; but just because of that, man cannot get away from his responsibility by suicide.

Q.: I have been trying to find out whether Gurdjieff was inspired a great deal by Christ because it seems to me that a lot of the things that have been said by Gurdjieff Christ has said to us in a different way, and if we could have understood what Christ taught, we should have been helped on our way a great deal.

J.G.B.: What I have said to you tonight may have sounded very different from what you read in "The Sermon on the Mount." It is not really different. When Christ said that the ax is laid at the root of the tree and that every tree that bringeth not forth good fruit is hewn down and cast into the fire, he was speaking about the same thing as I have been speaking about. Of that I have no doubt at all. But we have not understood what Christ taught. It is much worse than not understanding. Even what we have understood we have not done. If we had done any of the things that Christ taught, the whole world would be different today.

Q.: Do you think there is another reason for our existing than the one that you have given, that of serving a higher being?

J.G.B.: Reason is connected with responsibility, not only with need. Of course there is a responsibility toward what is lower, but if there were nothing higher, then it would not be a reason. You must know this, that by far the greater part of our human troubles comes from the fact that we do not feel ourselves responsible toward something higher than we are. To awaken to feeling *that* is the most necessary thing. This has been preached at people for thousands of years, and nothing has happened. Therefore, people have to wake up to it somehow; but until people begin to feel responsible toward something higher than themselves, they will always go on destroying everything, including themselves also.

Q.: I am puzzled by one of your answers. The question about suicide—that this is not the end of that individual and that something carries on, in spite of annihilation of everything that can be described anatomically and physiologically. If this is not his soul, is there any evidence for the existence of this other thing that goes on, any more than there is evidence for his soul?

J.G.B.: It is that in us which dreams. It is not the soul. The usual view of the soul as an independent, animating principle existing in the body is a relic of an old mistake—so old that no one can say when it was first made. People have perpetuated that mistake without making a real effort to find out what the supposed "soul" could really be. There can be a soul in man, but it is precisely that which could be present in a man who does not dream but *is what he is*.

I think that is enough for tonight. Many of your questions will be answered in later lectures.

"The whole individuality of every man… must already at the beginning of his responsible life—as a condition of responding in reality to the sense and predesignation of his existence as a man and not merely as an animal—indispensably consist of four definite distinct personalities."

—*All and Everything*

The Human Organism
and Its Functions

Lecture 2: March 15, 1954

 TRULY, I AM SURPRISED to see so many people here again today because I think that if you could really understand what I am trying to say to you, you would run away and not come back. Because, inevitably, if you understand what I am saying, you will have to lose very much of your wool. Our wool is our comfortable self-satisfaction. It is only given to us for a time; afterward, we shall be sheared. Maybe if you did really understand and had a strong enough heart, you would still wish to go through with it because it is better to be sheared than to be destroyed; and if we are not prepared to give our wool, we shall have to give a good deal more than our wool.

Tonight I want to speak about the human organism; that is, the living body of a man. Now if I were to ask you, "To whom does this body belong?" you would probably say it belongs to this man. But who is this man if he is not his body? If I am to say "my body," then I must be something different from my body. If I say "my horse," I know what I am speaking about because I can distinguish between the owner and the owned. But if I say "my body," can I distinguish it in the same way? If so, who is the owner or master in me who says "my body?" Let us ask ourselves that question as seriously as we can because you know that one of our great weaknesses as men and women is that we question, but we question rather lightly and do not drive our question right through to the end. Very few people are ever born who are able to push their questioning through to the end. Such people change the whole course of human thought. For most of us, our questions remain unanswered, and, after a time, we cease to care. However, even if we wish to answer them, we find we cannot do so alone. Maybe we have some chance if we will share our search with others, but even so, to go right through to the end, in the search for answers, is a very rare thing for man.

I shall try tonight to go at least some way with you toward an answer to the question, "Who am I that can say 'my body?'"

Where shall we start? We ask the question in our minds, in our thoughts. Can I say that I am my thoughts, that the "I" who thinks is the owner of my body? We know well enough that our thoughts are not independent of our bodies. Our thoughts are the result of what is going on in parts of our nervous system. We do not even know how thoughts originate except that somehow they depend upon some stimulus to the very complicated network of nerves in our head brain. However we may look at our thoughts and however deeply we may study them, we never can find them separate from our brains, or account for their process, except in terms of what is going on in our brains. Our brain is part of our body. How, then, can we speak of our brain or its thoughts being the master of the body? Moreover, if I look at my thoughts and ask myself, "Where in these thoughts am 'I'," I never can find that I am my thoughts, for I speak of "my" thoughts as I speak of "my" body. I am no nearer to meeting a master of my thoughts than I am of finding a master of my body. If I think of my feelings, my emotions, my likes, my dislikes, my loves, my hates, my interests, and the rest, are they "I"? Are they the master? Again, I must say "no." First of all, they are just as much the product of the working of my nervous system as my thoughts are, only a different part of the nervous system, a part of which I am usually not conscious. Also, I know how much my feelings, all my emotional states, are a matter of chemistry, of what is happening to my sympathetic nervous system and the glands and blood vessels it controls. These are my body. They control my feelings, it is not my feelings that control them. In any case ,what are my feelings? Just a changing kaleidoscope with its ups and downs of likes and dislikes. Nothing in them can be a master. My seeing and hearing and touching, all my sense experiences, belong to the working of my nervous system and depend upon the outside world to stir them into action. How can they be "I"? How can they be a master? Wherever I look, and the more closely I look, the more sure I am that none of these things, neither thoughts nor feelings nor sensations nor anything else that happens in me, can be called "I." So there must be something behind all those. Let me look for it.

Wherever I look, I see only a blank, behind which lies emptiness. I have to be able to look patiently and sincerely, but the more patiently and the more sincerely I look, the more I am bound to see that I find nothing. Who, then, owns my body? If it is no one or nothing, then my body is like a horse without a master, that is, wild, irresponsible. This brings us back to what we were talking about last week. I may be irresponsible but I am still answerable. I may be wild but still I shall be caught. Because I am wanted for something, whether I like it or not. We have to understand this when we speak about the human organism. We have to realize that it cannot be a wild beast. Yet we cannot find in our own experience the someone who can say, "I am the master of this body." We observe only a succession of changing states, changing thoughts, changing feelings, not masters even of themselves let alone of the body. That is the first thing we have to understand about our organism. It is an animal that does not yet know its master.

Now I want to talk more about this animal, and what it does and what is expected of it, before I begin with you in the next two lectures to search for the master, to see who and how he can be. For this, I have to make a very important distinction in what we can find out about ourselves, a distinction that consists in dividing that which we can experience into three different parts or three different aspects. One aspect is what we *do*, all the things that go on in us. That we can call our function. In a sense, it is what we are for. Another aspect is what we *are*. What we are is not what we do but that which we *are*. We can never find it when we look for it. What we were looking for just now—"I"—is what we are, as distinct from what we do and all that happens to us. We cannot find this by looking for it. It has to be reached in another way. That which we are, we can call the aspect of being. The third aspect is a little harder to describe. All the time, we and everything else that exists are somehow working ourselves out, as if there were a driving force behind us, behind us and behind everything, compelling us to get on with being what we are, with doing what we do. Whether we are aware of it or not, this force is always acting on us. We can say it is what acts through that which we are to make us do what we do. That force I shall call the will. It has its own laws, quite different from those of being and function. About being and will, I shall speak in the next two lectures [*see* chapters 3 and 4 respectively]. Tonight, I want to speak only about the aspect of function; that is, what we do. And the reason for beginning with this is that it is all that we can *know;* it is this alone that we can find when we look. Function comprises all the things I have been talking about—the body itself, its thoughts, its feelings, its sensations, its movements, and so on. You see how I have turned the sentence around. It is not the body that belongs to the feelings, to the movements, and the rest of them but the thoughts and feelings and sensations and movements and so on that happen to this body of ours. They are what we have to study first of all. Let us begin with our thoughts.

What is thinking? Do *I* think? That means, is thinking an intentional act of something that is present here that can be called "I"? Anyone asked that question would probably say "Yes, it is. That is just what thinking consists of. It is *I* thinking more or less what I choose to think." But it is not so at all. As soon as I begin to look, I discover that I do not in any way choose my thoughts; they arise in me or, rather, something in me becomes aware of them. I notice and, if I look carefully, I see that they are there all the time, sleeping, waking, whether I am noticing them or not noticing them, always there is something going on. This process should rightly be called "dreaming." All the time, I and you and all of us dream. As long as we live, from birth to death, we always dream. That is the first visible function of man, by which I mean that it is perceptible to his own inner experience. Wherever he looks, he finds dreams in himself. Not only man but all animals also dream. The cow that lies and chews the cud dreams. There is only one difference—but a very important one—in the dreams that man has; that is that the apparatus that is given to him for dreaming is much more complicated than the dreaming apparatus of other animals. There is an extraordinarily rich mechanism, a rich storehouse in his head brain, the midpart of his brain, with its thousands of millions of cells and tens of thousands of millions of connections between them, in which all the time this dreaming process is going on. Its presence can even be detected by the various means that science has discovered.

The content of the dreams is always being nourished, being filled with impressions that are coming from outside—what we see, what we hear, what we touch, all these things are giving us food for our dreams. The greater part, by far the greater part, goes on altogether inside us, repeating over and over again, repeating the impressions we received, especially the impressions we received in childhood. We are so constructed that we sort out and arrange these impressions, again especially in childhood, and collect them, as it were, into bundles, and we learn partly by imitation, partly by being taught, to connect these bundles of impressions with certain signs; first of all, certain sounds and afterward visual signs. The sounds are words and the visual signs are writing. Then all of these in their turn become material for our dreams, so that instead of dreaming like animals, almost entirely in pictures, we dream also in words. This makes our dreaming much more complicated, but it doesn't change its character. This is one thing that we have to see because, on the whole, people are not accustomed to recognizing that what they call thinking is only this automatic dream play.

There are, of course, differences between sleeping dreams and waking dreams. We sit here and dream together, but there is something that connects what is going on in my dreams with what is going on in your dreams. Waking dreams are different from the way we dream at night. Later, when I come back to this, I will explain to you how it is possible to change our dreams, to make of them something else than just an automatic daydreaming, such as most of our lives consist of. I refer not only to the reverie that we have when we are outwardly doing nothing but the greater part, nearly all, of our activity that proceeds with this dreaming present in us. All this forms a group of habits. I have spoken about some of the habits, such as the habit of collecting impressions into bundles and connecting them with words. We acquire by constant repetition other more complicated habits that constitute our ideas, opinions, convictions, and, in general, the whole content of our mental knowledge. Our awareness of all this elaborate dream activity varies very much. We have quite simple mechanisms in our head brain—the cerebral cortex—and in the ganglia at the base of our skull that prevent us from being aware of more than a tiny part of what is happening at a given moment. The whole apparatus is the thinking brain or, as Gurdjieff called it, the thinking center. The dreaming mechanism that is the basic structure of the intellectual center he calls the formatory apparatus because it is the means by which the formation of habits connecting impressions proceeds incessantly in us. The work of the formatory apparatus constitutes a considerable part of the activity of our organism.

We have another independent group of habits not formed in quite the same way; that is, not formed by the dreaming process but chiefly through a mechanism for imitation that exists in man by which he imitates everything. All animals have this mechanism more or less developed, some quite highly but man very highly. The mechanism is situated chiefly in his spine, in certain of the big ganglia at the back of his head and in the lobes in the front of his head. From birth onward, this mechanism, by the process of imitation, picks up all sorts of habits from the behavior of others around man. There is also implanted in this apparatus, even before birth, a whole lot of prepared, what we can call atavistic or innate, habits, the particular shape of which, in each one of us, comes from our heredity—what we can also call our instincts. They are habits handed down from generation to generation and can be called the genetic constitution of man. They are what is transmitted through the mechanism of heredity. There is a third mechanism at work, that of adaptation. The organism, the organism of man or of any other animal, has a power or property of adapting itself to the shocks that come to it from its environment, from other animals, and from other beings like itself. Between these three mechanisms, that is, the heredity or genetic constitution, the power of imitation, and the power of adaptation, a series of habits is formed by which our bodies acquire a certain pattern of behavior.

This pattern of behavior has three main parts: one is connected with the inner life of the organism that can be called the instinctive pattern, and is that Gurdjieff calls the instinctive center; another connected with all the outward actions by which we adapt ourselves to the world around us, and act on it, and all that is the motor pattern or, as Gurdjieff calls it, the moving center; and there is the whole activity of the sex function in man that Gurdjieff calls the sex center. These three together make the organic functions of man. Now the interesting thing about it is that they manage virtually the whole of the life of man, leaving what goes on in his head free to occupy itself with its own dreams—so that people live really two lives: one a life in which, by a whole series of prepared habits, their bodies are moving about and obtaining what is necessary for their nourishment, responding in complicated ways to all the situations that arise, and another a life, another world in which they simply dream. There is very little connection, and that chiefly accidental, between these two lives.

This is not very easy to accept because we suppose that many things are done with our head brain that are really done with these physical habits of ours. We don't notice, for example, that we scarcely ever talk with our heads. We nearly always talk with our motor mechanism, which, in fact, directly controls the organs of speech, and manages the whole thing very well, so that we can talk, even quite grammatically, even quite sensibly, and never think what we are saying. That means we never ask ourselves what it means; we never connect what we are saying with a picture, with an inner vision of the significance of it all; and we go through all our lives—and even remarkably well, considering—without thinking what we are doing. Neither we nor anyone else notices this.

In addition to these two lives of man, there is a third life that also is always present in him, one that is connected with another part of his nervous system, namely, all that part of the nervous system that is distributed over the body, in various nodes or ganglia, and especially in the region of the breast, the region of the solar plexus. This includes what we call the sympathetic nervous system and all the mechanisms that regulate the chemistry of our blood, which, in turn, is controlled by the state of the blood itself. This apparatus constantly registers our general state. In one sense, it is like an inner thermometer that is constantly comparing present experiences with the stored-up memories of other experiences. In that comparison, we are either making a movement of acceptance or a movement of rejection, a movement of expansion or a movement of contraction. That expansion and contraction communicates itself to our body and to our blood vessels, and so we experience unpleasant and painful feelings with the contraction and pleasant, joyful experiences with the expansion. All these processes constitute what we call the emotional or feeling life of man. All his likes and dislikes, all his pleasures and sufferings, all his desires and aversions are but the reflection in his experience of these movements of expansion and contraction in his nervous system and the changes that go with them in the chemistry of his blood. The mechanism that controls the feeling life of man is called by Gurdjieff the emotional center. This is a very sensitive organ; it knows, as it were, the temperature of our condition long before the dreams in our head begin to be affected by it, so that it can often happen that with an emotional shock, we become aware of the shock, we become aware of the change in the chemistry of our blood and the contraction of our blood vessels before we know what it is all about.

Of course, our dreaming part comes under the influence of this feeling part, which has certain important means of influencing directly the color and taste and the quality of our dreams or thoughts. The sympathetic nerves can pour their influences directly into the cerebral hemisphere by means of innumerable fibers connecting them with all the sensitive nodes distributed over the body. The nerves of the head brain in their turn react outward to produce corresponding movements and actions.

Going into it more in detail like this, you may see better why I said at the beginning that however we may look into all these processes, we cannot and never shall find anything that we can call "I" but only find a set of machines at work: electrical machines, chemical mechanisms, and so on. This should not surprise us at all if you followed what I was talking about last week [*see* chapter 1], when I said that man exists in order to transform energy that is needed for some purpose quite unconnected with his own personal existence. These brains, or centers, in us are very well adapted for the transformation of different kinds of energy. One kind of energy is transformed in our dreams, another in the whole activity of our bodies, and another again in our feeling reactions. All this happens to us whether we like it or not, and whether we like it or not depends solely upon the conditions of our emotional part. I say that this is all that we can find when we study man from any aspect that you like, from the point of physiology or psychology or by simply asking ourselves the question "Who am I?" and persisting in looking for the answer. We must accept the conclusion that is reached in that way, that there is nothing that we can find anywhere except these processes of energy transformation. Moreover, we can be quite sure that these energy transformations are not going on just for our benefit. On the contrary, we simply submit to the action of them.

If we say that this organism of ours is no more than an apparatus for transforming energy, then you may ask: What, then, is a man? You would be right to ask that question because certainly if we mean anything by the word "man," we do not mean a self-acting mechanism but a being somehow responsible, somehow able to direct—a being who is the master of something and especially a being who is the master of this organism, this body here. That is what we must mean if we use the word "man," and if we find nothing like that, then we are not entitled to use the word "man" as applied to ourselves. Are we then not entitled to use the word "man" at all? We are, providing we understand that it refers not to what we find when we look but to what should be there. What could be there is a being able to say "I," a being able to be the master of all this. Only such a being can say "I am a man." Before anything else, we have to realize that we are not able to say "I am a man" if we can find nothing except the functional mechanical mechanisms of which I have been speaking. Here we must not deceive ourselves. It is much too serious a question to get out of it by words, unless we are sure what those words mean, or just by refusing to think about it.

In the passage that I quoted at the beginning of this lecture, it is said that "Every man must as a condition of responding in reality to the sense and predesignation of his existence—as a man and not merely as an animal—indispensably consist of four definite distinct personalities." I have spoken about three, and when Gurdjieff says four, he means a fourth that is not included in these. In this passage, he goes on to describe the three personalities, the one that arises through dreaming and through sense impressions, that is, our thinking center; that which arises from heredity, imitation, and adaptation, that is, our moving, instinctive, and sexual selves; and that which arises in us by our sensitiveness to the passing state, that is, our feeling self. These are the first three. The fourth is that which in a man should be able to say "I." Of that, he says that without that fourth part, no one can call himself a "man." How can there be an "I" in man that is not all these things that we have been talking about?

I said at the beginning of this lecture that if you understood what I was saying, you would run away. Fortunately, perhaps, it is impossible for you to understand without a lot of experiment and observation and verification. So for the moment, we must talk as if you had done all that. If you had done all that, you would have seen that it is quite impossible to connect "I" with our thoughts or anything that happens in our thinking part. What we call our thoughts are nothing else but awareness of this dreaming process over which we have no control at all, and you would find that it is equally impossible to say "I" about any of the other parts either: I am not all my inner instinctive reflexes, I am not all the acquired habits of my external movements, all my behavior in the world; I am not my sexual impulses; I am not, either, my feelings, my thermometer. To understand how there can be "I," we have to learn something more about energies. Really, it would be very difficult if it were not that the distinctions that apply to our own inner world are also to be found in everything that we study—I mean that distinction between visible and invisible energy.

All the things that we have been talking about are the visible transformations of energy. All that is necessary is to find a suitable type of apparatus to detect them, and we can find them, measure them, start and stop them, just as we could with any electrical apparatus or anything that man may construct, and, in fact, physiologists have discovered ways of influencing all these parts of our psychic apparatus in a really very remarkable way.

There is one kind of energy, however, that cannot be interfered with like that, which cannot be experimented with, because it is always out of reach. That is potential energy—the energy of what might be, of what might happen, as distinct from that which is happening. If we look at a great rock rolling down the side of a hill or at an avalanche, we see its motion; the energy is there living for us. If we get in its way, we know very well that there is energy behind it, but if we look at the same snow lying quietly on the mountainside, we do not see this, and if we touch it, it does not hit back at us. That quiet, invisible energy is the potential energy. We know it is there because we know very well that if that rock were to be dislodged, it would roll down the mountainside and the snow would be picked up by an avalanche, however quiet and innocent it might be, as it lay on the mountainside. Those of us who know a little bit about physical science know that all this is due to the presence of the potential energy field of the earth's gravitation, the pull, as it is called, of the mass of the earth on everything that is within reach. That pull is not visible. We cannot do anything with it and we cannot measure it as it is there but only when something begins to happen, for example, when a weight stretches the spring of a balance. The same applies to the energy of the electric field. Such potential energy has an eternal quality. For thousands of years that rock could remain on the top of the hill and there would not be the slightest diminution of the possibilities of its rolling down the hill.

Inside our own nervous systems, there are also states of potential energy, when discharges are not taking place across the boundaries that connect one nerve with another. Energy in that state is quite different from the energy of what is going on. However, it doesn't mean that it has no power. On the contrary, that is the form of energy that alone has true power, just because it does not participate and is therefore not used up.

Potential energy is produced through an interruption in the flow of sensible energy, just as a pressure builds up in a pipe through which water is flowing if we close a tap. We exist to transform energy and especially to build up a potential that can be used for another purpose. This is true of all animals, and each species is a marvelous apparatus for transforming energy. The construction of animal bodies can only be understood if we realize that this is why they exist and are made such as they are. The same applies also to man. The human organism is constructed not for the convenience of man himself but to ensure that he produces what is required of him. A factory is not built to amuse its managers or even to provide work for its staff but to produce goods for commerce. Unless it produces goods of a quality and a quantity that justify the expenditure upon wages and materials, it is a failure and sooner or later must be reconstructed or closed down.

Gurdjieff often compared man to a chemical factory that is here to produce substances of a certain quality and quantity; if it fails to produce them, the factory is shut down. We must recognize in this comparison the same logic and justice as in the saying of Christ: "Ye shall know them by their fruits; every tree that bringeth not forth good fruit is hewn down and cast into the fire." Although such sayings have been known and quoted for thousands of years, people have had only the vaguest idea of what is meant by the "fruit" that is expected from man, and they thought of it in terms of external work or outward behavior, disregarding another saying of Christ, who taught that "The Kingdom of Heaven is within you." It is through the inner experiences of a man that the transformation of energy is accomplished through which alone he can produce the fruits that are required of him.

From this it follows that our bodies must be made in order to serve as apparatuses for this transformation of energy. Such a view of the body goes against all our habitual ways of thinking. Biologists look upon the body simply in terms of its self-preservation and self-renewal. Believers in evolution trace its descent from some more primitive forms of life. Economists and socialists think only in terms of its needs and its capacity for work. Religious people look upon it as a vehicle in which the soul is temporarily housed. Some even regard it as the enemy of the soul, and they speak of deliverance from the body as the greatest blessing. Most people take it for granted and never ask themselves what it is for or what it might be able to give. All such views are wrong. Our bodies are not merely the result of a blind evolution nor are they created for the good of an immortal soul nor yet do they exist in order to satisfy our own impulses. They serve for the transformation of energy required for the reciprocal maintenance of all that exists, and they are marvelously well adapted to this purpose and to no other. We can therefore only hope to understand the construction and functioning of our own bodies if we remember that they are before anything else apparatuses for the transformation of energy.

Within the limits of the existing world, energy can neither be created nor destroyed. Our bodies cannot create energy but they can change its forms, that is, its quality. Since the body cannot create energy, it must be supplied from outside with the raw material for its transformations, which is why Gurdjieff compares it to a chemical factory. The raw material that enters the body for the purpose of transformation is what we call food. Energy capable of transformation enters our organism in three quite different forms: the first is the food we eat; the second is the air we breathe; and the third is the impressions received through our senses. I shall not speak tonight about these different kinds of food nor about the primary stages of transformation that proceed automatically through our organs of digestion and in our blood and our nervous system. These primary transformations are the same for man as for any other animal, and they consist in making out of the different kinds of food we eat various substances; that is, forms of energy that make our experiences and our activities possible.

To enable the "I" that should be present in us to exercise its function as the initiating, regulating, and coordinating factors in the work of the centers, it must have at its disposal potential energy of the requisite intensity and quantity. This is possible only by a process of inner transformation, which can occur only if we are prepared and able to withhold and preserve some of the energy that flows into the activity of dreaming, the automatic reactions of our bodies, and our states of feeling. Man is made so that this work of preservation can take place in him only by his own decision and choice. Man can be something more than an automatic transformer of energy, but in order to become that something more, he must choose to do so and be prepared to pay for it.

Now we have again some forty minutes for discussion. If you ask any questions about tonight's lecture, I will try to answer them.

QUESTIONS AND ANSWERS

Question: All past religions and philosophies have given merit to humanitarian principles. Has this anything to do with Gurdjieff's philosophy whatsoever? Does it gain anyone any merit? Do murder, rape, love, faith, and so on count?

J.G. Bennett: It is easy to answer "yes," but I would like to say also why that is. I said at the beginning this evening that it is very hard and very rare for anyone to go through with anything. The truth is that we men are in a much worse situation than we realize or like to realize. Our lives are not arranged for our own welfare. We are being used. However, that does not mean that the Higher Power is indifferent or hostile to us. On the contrary, it puts before us not only all the possibilities of fulfilling our obligations but, at the same time, the possibilities of gaining something for ourselves. The situation is such that the chance of any one man doing this alone is very small. For this reason alone, we need one another and must respect one another. We are like travelers lost in the desert who have almost no chance of surviving unless they keep together as a caravan. That is the first—maybe selfish—reason why we have to respect one another's existence and one another's needs.

There is a much deeper reason in it than that, which will become clear from what I shall be saying next week about being [see chapter 3]. In the depths of our being, we are not separated from one another, as we appear to be on the surface. It is only in this outward functional activity, of which we are speaking tonight, that people appear to be separated from one another. The deeper we penetrate into man, the more we find that we share not only in a common need but even in a common being. At the very core of our existence everything is united. There is a saying of Christ, the second commandment to man, that he should love his neighbor as himself. Gurdjieff often used to explain this commandment, saying that, first of all, it is a test for ourselves. When we put it to ourselves, can we understand what it means to love our neighbor as ourselves? We cannot because we only look at what is going on, and what is going on has insides and outsides. What is going on in me is outside of what is going on in you. We cannot penetrate into that and we cannot love that. We cannot love another's function as if it were our own, but what *we* are is not separate in this way. What *you* are and what *I* am are not really two different things shut away from one another, and as soon as I begin to experience and see that, then I begin to discover what is the meaning of the saying, "Love your neighbor as yourself." You never can love him as yourself so long as he appears to be outside of you. When you find him inside you, then you cannot help loving him as yourself.

I will tell you, I paused a long time to answer your question because I was inwardly hurt and shocked by it: it is so contrary to everything that Gurdjieff's Teaching stands for, to think that indifference to the welfare of others could be consistent with caring for our own.

Q.: You have described objectively, and I stress *objectively*, the three centers that make up our automatic responses and have stressed a fourth one that, if I understood rightly, would be the potential "I." I wonder whether the "I" is not just a subjective awareness of the three centers that differs in every individual, and the fourth potential one is not a direct outcome of these three other ones, which will be an individual in each case. Furthermore, total energy must be limited, and it is merely a process of transformation. For the fourth center, you have to withdraw the energy from the previous three. I would therefore tend to regard the fourth one as an integrated self. The three centers are not integrated insofar as most people are not aware of themselves and cannot be themselves.

J.G.B.: What this lady says is interesting. She is right in concluding that awareness of the "I" is the result of the integration of the experiences of the other three; but if I had said that, I would have also drawn your attention to the fact that, such as we are, these three parts of us, or these three centers, do not have the unified experience that is required, and therefore that process of integration does not take place. It cannot take place automatically. Something intentional has to be done in order to bring about the mutual impact of these three centers; only if this is done can the fourth arise. They have to stand in a certain relationship to one another.

Q.: You repeatedly use the term "I" seemingly as something representing the whole personality. Is it possible you are just using a verbal symbol that has no other significance?

J.G.B.: That is exactly what the word "I" amounts to as applied to man such as we know him, and I was at pains to say that wherever we look, we do not find any fact that corresponds to the word "I." But there is a possibility of disengaging something that is free from the rest, and if this is done, then it can be seen that this fourth is not merely a resulting experience—an onlooker of what is going on in the other parts—but a force. Therefore, when it is set free, it is entitled to have a name. It is more concrete than the others, which are, after all, only changing processes, never the same from one minute to another, provisional— because when the "I" is found, we see that it does not change, only we do not find it when we look in the way that we look for facts.

Q.: You asked earlier, Who is the master of "I"? but you have shown how all these centers are automatic. I am not sure that in asking, Who is the master of "I"? that you do not mean some force above us and, if so, whether that force is just pure energy or something more than that. Does it lie within ourselves to discover who the master would be or is it something outside us to discover?

J.G.B.: It is a very natural and right question, and the answer will be given in the fourth lecture [*see* chapter 4].

Q.: Is there a connection between the teachings of Gurdjieff with respect to the realization of the "I" and the information gained by Indian and Eastern yogis and others of a high order in their trances and religious experiences?

J.G.B.: Why not? It does sometimes happen, as I have said several times this evening, that a man will arise who has in him the power to go through to the end with his questions. Such a man is in the true sense a man of high order, that is, "one who is unified."

Everyone of us has our own measure. Most of us are very dependent upon the help of others, and I must tell you this, that we Western people have become very weak, very fainthearted in this search. One may go to the East and find people with stouter hearts than we have and who therefore arrive at something that we do not. We have to acknowledge that we are very fainthearted. How many of *you* would be ready to pursue such a search to the bitter end with the determination to find the answer? Too many things pull us away from it. Our life drags at us altogether too much. Because of that, we have to find something that can help us, such as we are, and that, in my opinion, is the really wonderful side of Gurdjieff's Teaching, that it is possible for us to follow it in our ordinary conditions of life. To go through with that, that is as near as anything can be to a miracle.

Q.: You said that we have no control over our thoughts. Could you tell us what happens when we appear to have some control? When one says to oneself, I must not daydream, I must think about such and such a problem. Is that illusion?

J.G.B.: Choice is one thing, control is another. If you say, I will think about such and such a problem, you cannot foresee what thoughts about the problem will enter your mind and so you cannot control the thoughts themselves. But, to a very limited extent, you can say "yes" or "no." The power of "yes" and "no" exists in every normal man. That is the first power that he should seek to strengthen in himself because everything turns upon it.

Q.: Referring to the question before the last, you did not make it clear whether you thought we in the West could reach the same high attainment as yogis and buddhas in our way of living without locking ourselves up in monasteries, and so on. I wonder if it is possible.

J.G.B.: We must leave out the word Buddha, which stands for a being of a different order. I left unanswered one part of that question, that is, can we, such as we are, in our western conditions of life, hope to attain the same sort of high achievements as yogis and buddhists without shutting ourselves up in monasteries? The real question—and it is a very real one—is, can we, being engaged as we inevitably are in the external activities of life, hope to accomplish this inner transformation? The answer to that is yes, not only can we, but this is even the really most favorable condition for us. Those of you who like the Eastern scriptures will no doubt have read the *Bhagavad Gita*. There is one verse that for some reason appears twice. It is the only phrase that appears twice and it says that it is better to follow one's own destiny, even if it is without merit, than to follow the destiny of another, however well it may be accomplished: *"Sreyan svadharmo vigunah panadharmat svanustitat."** That is the truth. What we have is

_____

*Bhagavad Gita, Book III, verse 35.

right for us. Our conditions are the conditions in which we are placed to do this work, and this work must be done under these conditions. They are not to be run away from. They are our obligations; nothing is gained by running away from obligations. Never. Some quiet, of course, some tranquillity is needed. A certain part of this transformation cannot go without peace, but one can find peace under all conditions. I remember many years ago, an Indian yogi, whom I really respected, was talking to me one evening. He was in London at the time, and was describing to me how in the middle of Bond Street this inner change had taken place in him; all the way walking down Bond Street up to where we met, this had not left him at all, and he was able to be completely immersed in this state that they call *Samadhi*. I have no doubt that what he told me was true, and I have since experienced such a thing myself.

Q.: The peace you have just referred to in your last sentence, is that the place of the "I" that one should aim at?

J.G.B.: It is the home of the "I."

Q.: One would then rise above one's inner conflict? In that sense, it would be the home of the "I"?

J.G.B.: Yes.

Q.: You have just mentioned that we should not try to run away from our obligations. Isn't it very difficult to decide what our obligations are?

J.G.B.: In such things, we can start very simply, just taking what, on any showing, are our obligations. The more we understand, the more we can see what our obligations really are. But we can start always by accepting the obligations of what can be called the common morality of mankind—that which always, among all peoples, is recognized to be an obligation. There are the obligations of family, toward parents, toward children. Those always have existed, and always will exist, among men. There is an obligation to fulfill the task that life puts in front of me.

I speak now just about our functional existence, the things we do. Each one of us is in front of some task to be accomplished. These are our first obligations, needs to be looked after, and they are exactly what I meant when I say we cannot run away from them.

In the middle of all this, there is a great part of our activity that is not committed in any way, a great part of every day that is not committed. Sometimes not long periods, but always some, that we can use differently. Afterward we can learn how to work through our obligations, how to make our obligations the very means by which we accomplish also the inner transformation. If I speak about the possibility of man of acquiring awareness of his "I"? I also have spoken all the way through, last week and this week, of what man has to do. He has to live, whether he likes it or not. Someone spoke last week about suicide. He cannot run away from life, even that way. Our obligations are much more binding on us than we think.

The demand that life makes is a legitimate demand, and it has to be fulfilled. In fulfilling that legitimate demand of life, though, we have also the possibility of accomplishing something quite different. That is really the answer to that question about monasteries. Insofar as the monastic life consists in rejection of the responsibilities of life, it is a false way. Of course, it need not be that. But I say insofar as it is a denial of life, it is false, because life is as legitimate as the highest consciousness. All serve the one Great Purpose, and we can no more reject and deny the life of our little finger than we can deny the life of the whole universe. Everything has its place.

We men can serve this Great Purpose differently according to the way we exercise the power of choice that is given to us. It does not mean that one way is legitimate and the other illegitimate. If you read Gurdjieff's book, *All and Everything,* you will see a most wonderful exposition of the absurdity of using such words as "good" and "evil" in relation to one obligation as against another. Everything is sacred, but we have the possibility of serving this *sacred* in different ways, and doing so in one way changes our own situation entirely. If I only give myself to life, then nothing remains to me except that, but if I run away from life, I may find myself in a worse situation still.

Q.: In connection with the process of thinking, you said something about the external forces. Is that the same thing as coming under the influence of the universal mind?

J.G.B.: I meant in a very simple sense that sense impressions coming from outside are all the time being transmitted to our head brain and starting new trains of association. Biological research has begun to discover some of the mechanism by which sense impressions are registered in the head brain and not upon our dream state. In referring to the "outside influences," I simply meant that our thinking is not an intentional act on our part. We do not choose our thoughts. They arise either from the accidental combinations going on inside our organism or from some equally accidental stimulus from outside. We cannot think what we choose to think. We can say at the most "yes" or "no" to a given thought. The nervous system of man is so constructed that there is no means by which he can do more.

Q.: If we cannot choose our thoughts, at least we can direct them, or, if not, how can we reach the "I" that we must reach? Unless we had some control over our thoughts, we could never direct them.

J.G.B.: You just try to direct your thoughts. This is not a question to be studied theoretically. It is something to find out. It is just inaccurate, badly directed observation of what happens that allows us to entertain the notion that we can direct our thoughts. We cannot direct them, but there is a something that nevertheless is possible, and it would not be fair if I were to leave it at that. We have the possibility of transforming the work of our dreaming mechanism into a power of imaging. Then that can give direction to thought, if one is able to do it, but first we have to acquire something that is able to do it.

Q.: Has the search for the "I" any connection with "losing our life to find it"?

J.G.B.: Last week, I said without death there cannot be birth, or without death there is no resurrection. We think that birth comes first and death afterward. It is not like that.

Q.: What is it that one has to sacrifice in order to build up the potential necessary for the "I" to be formed?

J.G.B.: I would be glad if there were many questions like that—for it points to the heart of our problem. Every choice of yes and no is an opportunity of sacrifice. Every *yes* can move in one direction, even small. Certainly, I have, first of all, to learn to see what "yes" is. I cannot begin with that because I will not know what are the "yes" and the "no" at any given moment. So first I have to learn something before I can come to the question of sacrifice. Supposing that I have learned in which direction my energy is wasted and in which direction it is preserved. Then in every situation, I have a "yes" or a "no" in front of me. It is the reiterated, repeated exercise of this power that, little by little, builds up something in us that can be the vehicle of our own "I."

"All the beings of this planet then began to work in order to have in their consciousness this Divine function of genuine Conscience."

—All and Everything

Chapter 3

Consciousness and Its Possible Transformations

Lecture 3: March 22, 1954

TONIGHT I am going to speak to you about a topic that thirty-four years ago had special importance for me personally—namely, the problem of reconciling belief in universal law with private freedom.

I had been a student of natural science, and I had absorbed a certain amount of the critical philosophy, and I saw that all this inevitably led to one conclusion—that is, that everything that happens is governed by inexorable laws and must therefore in some sense be determined. From the other side, we have our own human experience, a feeling of responsibility, the feeling that what we do matters. If, however, we can do nothing, if all our thoughts and feelings and everything else are only the result of electrical and chemical processes going on in our bodies and acting on our bodies, this conviction that what we do does matter is just an illusion—not even a cruel illusion because there is no one to be cruel.

I must tell you that when I was a very young man, this dilemma really tormented me, and it was only when I saw with conviction that there was a way out that didn't involve sacrificing belief in the order of nature—that is, a belief in universal law or compromising with the conviction of our own real responsibility—that I had some peace with this question. That, perhaps more than anything else, is what decided me, when I began to understand something about Gurdjieff's Teaching, that I would really apply myself to understanding it, and I have been doing so ever since.

You remember last week [*see* chapter 2] I spoke about the choice of yes and no as perhaps the most important thing for us. The question that I asked myself is, How can this choice of yes and no really mean something? It was only little by little that I began to understand the answer to this. Choice can only be real if there is more than one possibility present. To choose between turning my head to the right or to the left means something only if I have a possibility of doing either the one or the other.

What is a possibility? Last week, we studied what happens to the whole functional aspect of human life, as a sample of all that we see going on everywhere, and in all this there are no possibilities, it all has to happen as it happens. We think, we feel, we do what we have to think or feel or do. We are obliged to do so because our thinking and feeling and doing, our seeing and hearing, are only the result of what is going on in a physical mechanism, that is, our bodies. You may remember that I said when we have seen for ourselves how man works, even in broad outline, with his three main groups of functions, we find nothing but a machine, and I also said that all "possibilities" for man depend upon there being a fourth possibility present that we call his "I," and I said that "I" is bound up with potential energy. I want to say more about that now.

There are two worlds. One is the world of *facts* and the other the world of *possibilities*. In the world of facts, there are no possibilities; in the world of possibilities, there are no facts.

As I shall have much to say about "possibility" this evening, I want you to realize that I mean by this word something that really exists and is present here and now, even though we can neither see nor touch nor even think about it or know it. The world of possibilities is as real as the world of facts. Indeed, as I shall try to show you later, it is a more substantial world than that of facts, both because it does not change and disappear, as facts do, and also because it is much richer in what it contains.

It is very hard to grasp the truth that possibilities exist independently of facts and can even have power over facts. Science, for example, thinks that it studies only facts, but it cannot get away from possibilities. In one most remarkable branch of science in which great discoveries have been made during the past century, that is, embryology, everything points to the presence of an invisible and even unknowable factor that determines the way in which a plant or an animal shall be formed from the seed. This is the pattern of its possibilities, and that pattern is always present. Its effect can be studied quite concretely and with much precision in the development of an embryo. It is through this pattern alone that damaged tissues or even complete organs can be renewed. It is this pattern that keeps each plant or animal within the framework of its own species. If we try to think of this pattern in terms of "fact," we get lost, but we are equally lost if we think of it as something immaterial, a mere "tendency," or, as some people might call it, a spiritual or vital agency. The pattern of possibilities is as substantial as the body, but it is made, as I said last week, of potential energy, instead of energy in visible form.* Therefore, when I speak of two worlds, I speak of two quite real substantial modes of existence, very different from one another but each equally necessary for us to understand. Between the two, there is a border, a frontier, and across this frontier there can be an exchange, and it is across this frontier also that "yes" and "no" can really mean something. What does it mean to be in the presence of possibilities? I said just now that I can choose between turning my head to the right or to the left, if it is possible for me to do either. But when is this possible? It is possible when I am aware that something is pulling me this way and something is pulling me that way. If I am not

---

* Those who are interested in this question should study the books of Dr. Maurice Vernet and especially *L'Evolution du Monde Vivant and Hérédiée*

aware of it, what will happen has nothing to do with *me*, it has only to do with the working of my functions. *I* am there to the extent that I experience the presence of possibilities.

Is it one thing to be aware and another thing to have possibilities? Probably you would answer "Yes, one can be conscious without possibilities, and there can be possibilities without consciousness." But I say no, it is not like that. There is no separation between consciousness and possibilities. Consciousness is indistinguishable from the presence of possibilities. Unconsciousness is the same thing as the absence of possibilities.

When I am asleep, I cannot, except to a very limited extent, adapt myself to what is going on around me. My possibilities contract themselves until they become just my vegetative existence. My body continues to function as an organism. That very contraction of possibilities is the change of consciousness. As the possibilities withdraw, consciousness withdraws with them. When possibilities open again, consciousness reappears. This is something that you have to observe and verify for yourself because you have probably been accustomed to using the word "consciousness" as if it meant "knowing" what is going on. If you look more carefully, you can see that we can know what is going on and yet not be conscious. We do things all the time that would not be possible if we did not know what is going on, and yet we are not conscious of them. This is a simple truth that we can all of us verify as often and as thoroughly as we please, and we should do so because it is the way to understanding something that is most important for us. In Gurdjieff's language, it means that we are "asleep" and that we live our lives almost entirely in "sleep."

When we begin to grasp this, we learn to distinguish between knowledge and consciousness. I am only conscious insofar as something is possible, and something is possible when I am not altogether identified with or lost in what I am doing, what I am knowing, and so on. So when we spoke before about two worlds, the world of facts and the world of possibilities, I would say we are connected with the world of facts by our knowledge and with the world of possibilities by our consciousness. Possibilities *are*, but they are not always present. Their degree of presence varies from time to time and even from moment to moment, and with them our consciousness changes also, so that our consciousness is a measure of the amount of possibility present. Our ordinary waking consciousness suffices really for the possibility of the simple choice of "yes" and "no." It is that possibility that constitutes waking consciousness.

We can verify this if we notice—for example, in dreams—that as soon as we are able to say yes or no to what is present, we immediately begin to wake up. When we find ourselves unable to say yes or no in a dream, we are caught in the dream, we feel ourselves imprisoned in it. It is the same way in front of life. I said that we dream all the time. We are imprisoned in dreams, even in our so-called waking state. We have more possibility of escape, but that depends entirely upon whether or not we exercise the power that comes to us through the presence of the possibility of choosing. Wherever you look, you will see that possibilities and consciousness are inseparable. As what is really interesting and important for us is our possibilities, the study of consciousness is the key to real-izing our aims, all that is important for us in life.

Our functions must remain as they are. They belong to the world of facts, and from that world they cannot escape. Thinking remains thinking, feeling remains feeling, feeling, touching, and all the rest, remain what they are. However, consciousness can open and expand—even without limit.

If you can distinguish between the two states of consciousness in which the greater part, nearly the whole, of our life is passed, you can see that there is one sharp moment that we call "waking from sleep," at which the possibilities present change from one to two. In sleep there is only one possibility, that is, what is going on. When we awaken, two possibilities are present, those of yes or no. That is an enormous difference, and people quite overlook the fact that every-thing that matters to them and that can matter to them in life depends just on this.

The presence of two possibilities is still only a very limited form of con-sciousness. The whole situation has much more in it than that. My existence has much more in it than just the choice of yes and no at a given moment. When the pattern of my existence begins to be present to me, my consciousness is trans-formed. That is the second great transition.

It is the entry into the third state of consciousness, which Gurdjieff calls true self-consciousness. It is called self-consciousness because it is the presence of the possibilities that are in oneself. My choice then changes; it is no longer a choice only between two different directions in my functional activity but the choice of conforming to my pattern or not; of being what I am or not. That being what I am, the pattern of my possibilities, is what Gurdjieff calls our Essence. Essence-consciousness, the presence of the pattern of one's own being, is the condition for a real direction of life.

Just as our sleeping state and our waking state have gradations, so this third state has gradations also. It is a great and rare thing for man to be able to see the whole pattern of his life, to stand in presence of what he really is. He may have glimpses of it, glimpses sometimes so short that when he returns to his ordinary state of consciousness—the simple yes and no consciousness—he can no longer reconstruct what he has seen, except in a very vague way and by translating it into terms of what he can see, touch, think, feel, and the rest of it. He loses con-tact with what he is because to be in the presence of what one is is the third state of consciousness, and when we are not in that presence, we know only our func-tions and the immediate possibility of the moment.

There is one thing more I want to say, before I go on further, about the rela-tionship of function and knowledge to time and possibilities and consciousness to eternity. Our possibilities are not something that comes and goes; they are the pattern of what we are in eternity and can actualize or fail to actualize in time. Our consciousness also is not something that goes on; for what goes on, Gurdjieff uses the term "actualize" and speaks of actualization. All actualization belongs to the functions, that is, everything that goes on in time. Everything that goes on in time is subject to certain laws, the laws of time. Everything that doesn't go on, that simply is, is subject to different laws—also to laws, because nothing is without laws, but quite different laws. These are laws that are unknown, laws that science doesn't look for, but, little by little, they can be discovered if we learn how to examine our own experience. All that I have been saying about the different states of consciousness for man, the different ways in which possibilities are present, belongs to the laws of eternity.

To complete that picture, we have to make one more step; that is, to go beyond our own possibilities to *all* possibilities, to the whole pattern of everything. To be in the presence of that is a completely different state or form of consciousness. This is what Gurdjieff call the fourth, or Objective State of Consciousness. Then man stands not in front of his own pattern only but of the whole pattern of everything. Then he can see his place in relation to the whole. Then only he can really direct his life. So we can say that only a man who is able to be conscious in this way—that is, to stand in the presence of the possibilities of everything—is able to be free. He alone, in the full sense, is independent because he sees where he stands in relation to the whole. This is what Gurdjieff means when he says that only the fully transformed man can "do."

Of course, full experience of the fourth state of consciousness is unimaginable. We cannot picture to ourselves that any beings such as we are could ever stand in front of the pattern of All That Is. But here again, glimpses are possible, and we know that such glimpses have come to many people, who have tried to describe what they have experienced. Description is language; language means words; words, knowledge, and function all belong to fact; and in trying to bring the full dimension of All Possibilities into the world of facts, very much has to be left out. Inevitably, descriptions become, as it were, factual descriptions. One would expect that such descriptions would be hopelessly confused and contradictory and that no two people would ever say the same thing about what they had seen when they were in the presence of the Pattern of All Possibilities. Truly the extraordinary, even miraculous thing is that there is so much consistency. When we read the descriptions left by the great mystics, we feel that something is being said that refers always to the same reality, however the words may differ.

Such experiences lead us to believe that it is possible for man to get beyond the limited pattern of his own possibilities and see something that is quite different from a knowledge of facts, quite different from the conviction of reality.

I have told you about the Four States of Consciousness, indicated in terms of the presence of possibilities. There are other ways of indicating them, but to me, this is what shows most directly how fact and possibility can be connected with one another and, therefore, how we can hope to do something about our situation because if there were two entirely separate worlds, and all our ordinary experience were inevitably imprisoned in one of them, the reality of the other would not mean very much to us. However, before I can speak about what is open to us in the way of entering the world of possibilities, I must talk about something that you may or may not have noticed. I have said that possibilities and consciousness are inseparable and that possibilities are eternal—therefore, they certainly do not come and go and must always be present—and yet our experience of consciousness is usually restricted to a very small "presence of possibilities." How can that be?

Those of you who have read Gurdjieff's book, *All and Everything,* will have noticed that he frequently refers to one consciousness in which a man passes most of his waking state and another consciousness that is usually called the unconsciousness, which he calls the real consciousness of man. He says many very important things about this real consciousness.* If these passages puzzled you, then you should have insisted with yourself in asking, What can this mean? How can the real consciousness of man be unconscious? If you had insisted on finding an answer to that question, you would have probably seen what I am going to say now; namely, that the *real consciousness of man is the presence of the whole of his possibilities.* That consciousness always exists; but we, in our usual state, are isolated from it because we are trapped in the activity of our functions. We do not exercise the power we have of choosing "yes" rather than "no," so we remain with all the "no-possibilities." We remain shut up in a "no," and this "no," in which we are shut up, we call our "consciousness." It is the passive part of our existence, the functional part of our existence, that is altogether oriented in time. The peculiar thing about our human existence is that from childhood we are taught, and we learn, to say no to everything that is real and yes only to that which is imaginary; therefore, we develop an almost unconquerable habit of living in "nos." **

We do not think of them as "no," of course; we think of ourselves as very affirmative because we say "yes" to what we want, we say "yes" to our impulses, and we think that this is some kind of affirmation of what we are. But it is acceptance of dreams, and if we study our own childhood, and that of any children growing up around us, we can see how, by every means, we and they are led to accept, and to prefer to exist in, the dream state. The one thing that everyone without exception impresses on children is the need for insincerity, the need to appear to be other than what one is, to hide what one is and to appear different. No parent, no teacher, ever does anything else with children. All companions, all the surrounding influences have this effect. Thus there is a progressive shutting out of all the experience of possibilities, and their replacement by dreams, and, with dreams, just living in the functional life only. That is the situation in which we all find ourselves now, so that we hardly believe in our possibilities or we misunderstand them so badly that we think that they are the same thing as our dreams.

The result of this is that man gets divided into two parts. He gets shut up in the world of facts and shut out of the world of possibilities. The world of possibilities is always there, and it is there that his real consciousness is. We inevitably discover, if we begin to study man as psychologists do, that there are very powerful forces present in him that do not enter into his ordinary consciousness, and psychologists have even discovered that these forces are the ones that govern his

---

* Compare [c.f.] for example, *All and Everything,* p. 359.
** c.f. *All and Everything,* p. 147.

possibilities. For the most part, though, they look upon these forces as belonging to some inferior, more primitive part of man—either a remnant left over from a brutish ancestry or else as something half-formed in him that, in either case, interferes with his normal life. When the effect of these hidden forces disturbs his ordinary life, their one anxiety is to remove this disturbance and restore him to normal conditions; that is, where he is content with the world of facts.

Real normality, real sanity for man is to look for what he is, not simply for what he does. What we are is our consciousness. Our possibilities are what we are—not our actualization, which is merely what happens to us. It is our possibilities that hold us together. Without possibilities, everything is atomic, a lot of unconnected processes. If we study this, it is very interesting to see how, throughout all existence of which we are able to learn something, it is the possibilities that hold things together, not the facts. Even in an atom, even in the simplest thing of all—that is, an atom of hydrogen—it is the possibilities that hold together its two parts. It is by a certain mutual surrender of possibilities, in which one part gives up something of its possibilities to the other, that a stable whole is produced. We also, as men, are subject to the need to reconcile possibilities with facts.

That brings me to the question about which I spoke earlier. How is something to be done about all this? What is the connection between the world of facts and the world of possibilities? We men and women can find this link in us in one strange and very important property, that is, the property of attention.

Attention is the meeting point of what is actual and what is possible. With my attention, I am able to stand on that frontier between the two worlds. It is through attention that I am able to choose. Attention is not the same thing as consciousness and attention is not the same thing as knowledge, but attention links the two together. It belongs to consciousness, it belongs to knowledge, it belongs to possibilities, and it belongs to facts. Now there is in man one special organ that is sensitive to the presence of possibilities, to the balance that there is between that which is possible and that which is actual in a given situation, and through this organ he has the power of living at the frontier of the two worlds. This organ is quite well known to physical science. It is the cerebellum, the big bundle of nerves at the back of the head, the purpose and role of which, in man and in other animals, is only slowly becoming to be understood. It used to be thought that it had very unimportant functions. Little by little, it is becoming clear that it is one of the master organs, and if you will read Gurdjieff's *All and Everything,* you will see that he stated the role of this organ in man long before comparatively recent research by physiologists began to make this apparent. Through this organ, we have a measure of the possibilities that are present in relation to the facts that are present. Therefore, it determines the power of attention at a given moment. I said it is one of the most important organs, and indeed it is so, but we do very little about developing its latent powers because in the ordinary way man does very little to study or to develop his own power of attention. Yet it is through that alone that he can cross over this frontier that leads from the world of facts into the world of possibilities.

Before continuing with attention, there is one last thing I want to say about the world of possibilities, the fourth state of consciousness; that is, about that state in which man finds himself in the presence of far greater possibilities than those of his own private existence alone. In this unconscious part of man, as we call it, which is his real consciousness—because it is there that his possibilities are—there is also a point of contact with the possibilities that are beyond his own private existence, his own personal being. This point of contact is the one guide to the ordering of life. It is only through this that man can see for himself what he has to do; it is only through this that something can return into his world of facts, his world of function, and adjust it to the world of being. This point of contact is what Gurdjieff calls Conscience. He also calls it the Representative of the Creator, because it is that point in ourselves where we can stand in the presence of the Possibilities of the Whole. About it he also says that, in spite of all that has been spoiled in the life of man, Conscience remains in him untouched; therefore, to find it again, and to be able with its aid to establish the true sense of our lives, is the secret of fulfilling the reason and significance of our existence because without Conscience, even if we could see the pattern of our own private existence, we still couldn't see how to adjust our own pattern to the pattern of the whole.

You may remember that last week I said, in answer to one question about our responsibility toward our fellow men, that in the depths of our being we are not divided. In Conscience all are the same; all of us in our Conscience touch the same place and are open to the same world. This means that people can understand one another and their lives can be harmonized, but only to the extent that they are able to be open to their Conscience. I said *our* Conscience; I should have said "conscience" because it is not a private possession of any one of us. That of which I can say "I," "you" is the way to it—the way that we have to find in ourselves. Attention is the extraordinary instrument that is able to make that journey, a journey that must always go through uncharted territory because no knowledge will help us in this journey to that part of ourselves where we are able to stand in front of the possibilities of the Whole. Although that vision of the Whole is very remote from us such as we are now, something can nevertheless be transmitted to our ordinary state. It may help us to see this if we compare Conscience itself to the light of the sun. Some light passes even through the thickest clouds, and because of this light, everyone is sensitive to the need to find Conscience. However much we may run away from what it implies, and however much we have been encouraged, and encouraged ourselves, to prefer dreams to reality, something in us cannot be quite at peace with that. That "not quite at peace" state presents itself to us in the form of some question. If we face that question with the determination to find an answer, we are led step-by-step to the point where we realize that it is not in what we do but in consciousness of what we are that the transformation has to be accomplished.

Something has to be built in us that is able to be a bridge between the worlds. I said that we are prisoners in the world of facts. I did not mean by this to suggest that the world of facts is one from which we can escape. Actualization is as necessary a part of the Great Reality as possibilities. We cannot escape from actualization, but we need not be wholly imprisoned in it. Man can travel, he can move from one world to another; and, what is more—if this bridge is built—he can live in both the worlds, and then only can he fulfill what I was talking about in the first lecture [*see* chapter 1]; that is, his obligation toward the whole exchange of energies—the whole transformation of energies—and, at the same time, enter into his whole possibilities and become what he really is. Don't forget for the purpose of all our future discussions that the key to this, and the instrument, is our attention. It stands there between those two worlds—an instrument that we have to learn to use if we wish to come to any of these things about which I have been speaking.

There were one or two questions that were asked in letters by people who had been to the last lecture. It may be that some of you may also wish to ask questions that have occurred to you since last week. Others may like to speak about what I have said this evening. You must understand that in one hour, I can give only a bare sketch of an idea. Each of these ideas is very big, very full of meaning, and in sketching them out before you like this, necessarily very much is left out. To fill that in is a big task, which we may start with the help of your questions.

QUESTIONS AND ANSWERS

Question: Do you consider that conscience is acquired or innate? In that connection, you said that we educate our children so as to bring them up to say "no" to everything instead of "yes" to what you call their dreams and I call their instinctive pride. Is that inherence—which I agree is a bad one—to say "no" to many things not an attempt on the part of the parent to bring about a conscience in them, which I consider is not innate? Also, do you think conscience in different races or tribes varies considerably?

J.G. Bennett: What you call conscience is simply a group of functional habits, just the opposite of [what Gurdjieff calls] "Conscience." Not only is Conscience innate but it is something more than that. It is universal and unvarying, not only the same for different people but the same at all times. If there were beings on other planets, Conscience would still be the same for them as it is for us. That is so, simply by definition because I say that Conscience is to stand in the presence of the possibilities of the whole. What you call conscience is what one can call tribal morality. It is only functional. That is taught, and that is really one of the things that prevents people from coming to the real Conscience. It is a temporal substitute for an eternal reality. One morality can contradict another morality, but there can never be any contradiction in Conscience.

Q.: Would there be any connection between the patterns of possibility for different people or are we all entirely unique?

J.G.B.: There are three answers to that. One part of us is entirely unique, one part of us is all mixed up, and one part of us is the same for all. That means that there is one aspect of our nature that is higher than individuality, one aspect that is lower, and one part that is individual. About that I will speak next week [*see* chapter 4].

Q.: Could you tell me about the development of the cerebellum in a baby? Is it born fully developed or does our education develop it? Is it an automatic process or is it a result of the child paying more attention to its surroundings as it grows older? Do we in fact retard the development of the cerebellum?

J.G.B.: If you are speaking of the power of attention, then it is something different from what I said about the "no attitude." Attention has itself different qualities. There are fine qualities of attention that do not enter into ordinary life at all. They have to be elicited, developed by a special kind of experience, and they require also experience of life. It does not mean that a child could be so trained that it would have from the start these fine qualities of attention. It is necessary to have passed through life in a certain way—to have experienced, to have tasted, and out of that taste to make something. Therefore, it is not the fault of parents that children do not acquire this fine kind of attention; that is another matter. When I said we do everything to produce the preponderance of the denying element in man, I mean this—that we bring everything to the level of function. If you ask yourself how much do we care about what we, or children or anyone else, *are* or how much do we care about what others *seem to be*—that is, what they do, what they look like—and really ask yourself that question, what will you be obliged to answer? What is all life based on—but really all life—except what appears and not what is? That is what I mean by saying that everything is on the side of denial because what appears to be is the denial of what is.

Q.: I am terribly puzzled by the use of the word possibility, which has recurred all through the lecture. Do I take it that if you use the faculty of attention you get into touch with your own pattern? That is an end in itself. Does attention not imply actuality, and does pattern not imply a carrying out, or do I take it that the pattern is more important than the carrying out and the possibility is more important than the actuality?

J.G.B.: That was very clear, wasn't it?

Q.: Do you attach no importance to conduct?

J.G.B.: That you can hardly ask, after all I have said about our being obliged to live in the world of facts, which is the world of conduct. It is the world to which we have a responsibility. It is not that one is more important than the other but that all life is so overweighted in the direction of facts that, in order to redress the balance this evening, I had to speak about the neglected side. It is not a question of escaping out of the world of facts into a world of possibilities. That is nonsense. Neither facts alone nor possibilities alone make a full, make a complete man. It is the marriage of the two. Facts without possibilities are sterile. They are just the life of a machine. Conduct, if it is nothing but automatic reaction to stimulus, is neither interesting nor significant conduct. Only conduct that is based on choice in front of possibilities is significant. You remember I said at the beginning that everything for man turns on the choice of "yes" and "no." That choice of "yes" and "no" is something he does; it is the entry of his possibilities into his functions. Only he cannot choose unless the possibilities are there.

However, possibilities alone are no more insignificant than facts alone. There is no more to be gained by turning one's back on the world of facts than there is by turning one's back on the world of possibilities. Turning one's back on the world of facts means, in effect, to surrender oneself to dreams. We have to do something with the power that should be concerned with our possibilities; and when I said last week [*see* chapter 2] that we live in dreams, that is what I meant—that where we should be facing possibilities and choosing responsibly, we only dream and let things go on automatically. That can only be called "conduct." Real conduct begins where the attention links the possibilities with the action; in other words, where one chooses—seeing what one is choosing. You understand? (No.) Please ask more. Don't be satisfied.

Q.: I think your lecture shows the limitation of words. I feel that with these things words are disguising what you are trying to say instead of revealing it. I wonder whether the word "possibilities," which is deliberately puzzling, means the same thing that by people with similar experience, has been called ultimate reality, which to me seems to convey far more.

J.G.B.: Except that it is not relative, whereas possibilities are relative. You must allow for the relative in this. The reason I chose the word "possibility" is this: that the simplest situation is the one where there are just two possibilities. No question arises here of ultimate reality, just two possibilities, "yes" or "no," at a given moment. It is necessary to study for oneself, to look into oneself and see how I can make this choice of "yes" and "no."

Q.: You were talking about the similarity of described experiences, experiences that have been described by people who have them in a way that those who know about them can recognize them. This is more than a possibility. Do you think what Socrates described as his demon or guiding spirit, or what Brother Lawrence* described as presence—is that what you mean by conscience?

J.G.B.: Our problem is to see how to go, step-by-step, from where we are toward a goal. Sometimes it is easier to speak about the goal than about the way. There is an aim, there is something toward which we can strive. We may describe that in different ways, but our problem is to know how to move from where we are—to find a way by which we can speak to one another about how to make a step. That is what we need.

Q.: I have two questions. The first is whether or not this process you describe ever reaches finality. The second refers to last week's talk: monasteries, ashrams, and so forth. You said our work was here, in the world of actuality. You also spoke of a state of consciousness, *Samadhi* and referred to one of your friends from India. I believe that it is necessary at certain stages to go away or leave the world of actuality for a time, and try to discover and experience a state of possibilities that will lead to nonfinality.

J.G.B.: There is for each one of us at a given moment a limit beyond which we cannot go. Each one of us, such as we are, can reach a certain point, but we

---

* *Cloud of Unknowing.*

don't do that; for the most part, we are lazy in respect of what is possible for us, and therefore we do not stretch our boundaries. From that, we are inclined to think, "If my conditions were different, then I would be able to do it." We find a voice saying in us, "If I were to go away from the world of actuality and occupy myself solely with this question, then I would stretch my boundaries and I would be able to penetrate more deeply." There is something dangerous about this. It does not at all follow that by removing the pressure of the world of facts that it becomes easier for us to enter the world of reality. There is a great danger then of simply entering a world of dreams.

Q.: You talked about a certain state of consciousness or a state of awareness and withdrawal. There are many aspects in reference to this point. While immersed in London, a world of actuality, I experience myself surrounded by the noise of people. On the contrary, the same experience in a world of peace ...

J.G.B.: I said before, and I say again, that without some peace, this journey that I have spoken about—journey in consciousness—cannot be made. If one is altogether taken up with facts, activities, actualization, one cannot make it. But it doesn't mean that one has to go a long way in order to find peace. It is one of the mistakes that we all of us make—of thinking that if only my conditions were different then I could do something that I can't do now. Really, it is not like that. We can have the peace that is necessary for this work in the midst of this life. I don't say that some withdrawal is not necessary, but no withdrawal that involves a sacrifice of our obligations. I say again, as I have said every evening, that we have obligations in this life, in this world of facts, and those obligations we cannot escape. Thus, we have to learn how to gain the other while fulfilling the obligations to this. People who have thought otherwise have not contributed to solving our human problem, which is to be able to live as human beings, to serve one another, not to run away from one another. Our human problem is to be a human society, and for that we have to be able to be *what we are* in this society of ours, in this human family of ours, not withdrawing from it and repudiating it.

Q.: You have spoken of dreams. Is not consciousness all illusion, and if all consciousness is illusion, what does any system matter at all?

J.G.B.: The question is more difficult to answer than it looks. It is not sufficient to say that facts are not an illusion, and it is not sufficient to say that our feeling of freedom is not an illusion. The answer to it is that you have to wake up, and only when you wake up do you see what is real and what is illusory. If you ask, Who will guarantee to me that there is such a thing as waking up and that, if I were to wake up, things would be different? I answer, Nobody can guarantee it. No arguments can have the slightest conclusive force in reply to the question: "If it is all an illusion, what does anything matter?" It is a question that is beyond logic. The only answer to it is: If you have the courage to try then you may find. If you have the courage to look for reality, you may find it. You have a much better chance of finding it if you really understand that at present you have nothing to be certain of.

Someone asked me yesterday the question: "What can we rely on in ourselves?" In answer to that question, I said, "What happens when you breathe and the air goes out of your lungs and they are empty? You have to take air in. All other questions disappear beside that. If you have known what it is to be near suffocating, you know that all questions disappear beside it. You can rely on this, that as long as you can breathe, you will breathe. Why can we rely on it? Because it is a necessity. We need air. We cannot exist without it. The only thing we can rely on is that kind of an experience of need." If I need an answer to my question, if you truly needed an answer to the question that you have just asked—that is, to discover whether there is a reality where things matter—and if you needed the answer like you need air, then I assure you, you would find it. Really, you do need the answer just as much as you need air, only you don't know it.

Q.: Is consciousness something that exists or is it an abstract entity? Is it to be discovered by all and every one of us or is it a varying quantity that is personal for each individual?

J.G.B.: You remember I spoke about two states of consciousness beyond the ordinary, one of which Gurdjieff calls subjective and the other objective. They are very different in their significance for the ordering of our lives. To be open to the subjective state of consciousness alone is not sufficient to enable one to walk with certainty as to where one is going. Only when the objective state of consciousness opens can man be independent, relying upon what he himself sees. So that when you ask about either/or, I reply that the two halves of your question refer to the two aspects of the deeper consciousness possible for man.

Q.: Can you give us a practical example of the fourth state of consciousness referred to in the lecture?

J.G.B.: You may have read the discourses of [the Roman philosopher] Plotinus and the letters about him written by one of his friends and pupils—I think it was Porphyry. He says there that Plotinus had reached that state three times in his life—but Porphyry not once yet. If you study the discourses of Plotinus you can hardly doubt that he had indeed reached the fourth state of consciousness and derived many of his descriptions of the higher world from his memories of that experience.

Q.: Are the recent experiments of [the English novelist and critic] Aldous Huxley with mescaline the same thing?

J.G.B.: It is a natural question to ask. There is a whole variety of active substances that can either stimulate one function or put other functions to sleep. They are all very interesting. There are also substances that can bring a man into the third state of consciousness, even into the fourth, but they have the effect that afterward he cannot remember. Mescaline simply produces a normal functioning of the power of sight—a power that we use in a very clouded way, that is all. It enables people to see as it is natural for them to see, perhaps as they saw as children but have forgotten. Sometimes people are astonished that children draw some lines on paper or see something in nature that obviously they find quite significant and cannot understand why older people cannot see the extraordinary meaning that there is for them in what they have drawn. Maybe they are able to see in the way that is given by the use of mescaline.

Q.: My question has some relation to your last remark. You have been sketching a part that we may fulfill for the purpose of our existence, and most of us have been taxing our brains very fully to try to understand it. Is the kind of progress that you have in mind something necessarily connected with the intellectuality or do you think that people of very little education, very little brain power may achieve something of these things without necessarily understanding them? I might quote a child or [the French Martyr and Saint] Joan of Arc, who perhaps passed into the third or fourth state of consciousness.

J.G.B.: I must tell you this. If I have given you the impression that to follow these ideas requires a special intellectual development, then I have entirely misled you. It is not true at all. It is not very easy to speak about these ideas in a general lecture so as to give a picture of what it is all about, but when it comes to knowing what has to be done, what is the work, then everyone is equal, for it means that everyone has to start from the beginning. Too much mental baggage can even be a handicap. People can go on being stopped year after year because they can't think simply about these things.

Q.: Is consciousness better than unconsciousness and why does man have to seek for explanations of his existence? Why is he frightened to stand alone? Why does he have to give a reason for all this?

J.G.B.: Because man is not intended to live like an animal. Everything is wanted for some purpose, and man is wanted not only for what can be produced by the automatic transformation of energy of his automatic existence but for a higher purpose also, and for this reason something has been put into him that makes him ask questions. That something that makes him ask questions is his truly human part. The question, "Is consciousness better than unconsciousness?" means simply this: Is it better to be a machine just reacting to the influences that play on us or is it better to be a responsible being able to choose? I reply, "Neither better nor worse but different." Machines are also necessary. There is not any better or worse but simply the question of what I myself accept. Can I ignore this part in me that makes me ask questions? If I can, perhaps I am lucky. There may be something in a cow which makes her ask questions, but as far as we can see, she takes very little notice of it. It is possible for man to live like that also.

Q.: You said on a previous occasion that we are all on this earth and our object is to change radiations to higher powers, and you said this evening also that we each have a stage of development that we must reach and beyond which we cannot go. Has this difference to do with this power of radiation, or the transformation of energy, and how many people achieve this? Are there different stages? Do we have different possibilities, different aims for different people?

J.G.B.: I said this evening that there is a stage beyond which each of us cannot go, and you ask whether this is connected with the transformation of energy. I did not say there was a stage beyond which we can never go; I said that such as we are, at a given moment, there is a certain maximum possible for us, but that maximum can be increased if we choose. I even said, in reply to one question, that it can be increased without limit. The other part of the question was this,

Are there only a certain number of people who are able to realize their possibilities and therefore transform energy in a different way? That is really a very big question. It is the last one I shall answer this evening. Someone also wrote a letter after last week's lecture [*see* chapter 2] suggesting that I was talking as if there were only two destinies for man, either to be saved or to perish, asking whether that view does not lead to all the absurd divisions of the world into two categories of people only—the saved and the damned.

There are two parts to the answer to this question. First of all, that the transformation is relative, it is a process. If something is able to go beyond this life, then that something also must be capable of further transformation. Even if something is produced that is able to survive, it does not follow that that would be able to make the next step. Everything is relative; there are not just two categories but many gradations.

However, that is the least important part of the answer. The really important part of the answer is that *we are not alone.* This is not a private affair. It has been one of the great errors in the past to think that this is a private affair, that each person either goes to his own salvation or to his own damnation, irrespective of what may happen to others. Because of that, many terrible misunderstandings have entered into human life. The transformation is a task that we have to accomplish together, and those who can do more have to help those who can do less. To be able to do more is to have an obligation, not only to oneself but toward others. We are not a lot of atoms, each surrounded forever in its own private shell to reach, or not to reach, its own private destiny. It is not like that. We are intimately interdependent. We need one another not only from the outside but from the inside also. This dependence, this need for one another, is not just a need for mutual help. We need one another in order to be able to exist at all. Therefore, the fact that some have more power of work than others does not mean that they are the lucky few. Not at all. Simply that the greater burden is put on their shoulders, and if they will not carry that burden, it is very bad for them. The one really terrible thing in human life is to have the possibility of helping others and not to do it. Because of this close interrelationship, the whole conventional picture of saved and damned is false. But, of course, our life is generally false. We do not live recognizing these interrelationships. If ever a real life is to come for man, if ever this earth is to be what it should be, it will only be when people see this need for one another. Just as what I said before about air. If I realize that I cannot even breathe alone, then it is different, then I will feel differently toward my neighbor.

"The difference between what is called that 'I' which should be in the common presence of a real man and the pseudo 'I' which people to-day mistake for it."

—*All and Everything*

Chapter 4

Individuality—Fictitious and Real

Lecture 4: March 29, 1954

 As I come before you to speak, I experience each time a feeling of great compassion for our human situation. We have to talk together about the most important things that can concern us men and women, and yet we find ourselves imprisoned each in our own habits of thought, in our established points of view, and surrounded by words that, like prison guards, shut us in and prevent us from coming into an open ground where we can share a common understanding. The limitations of words and language are really a great handicap. We can, however, in addition to words, make use of the language of pictures, and I am going to try this evening to see if we can understand one another with the help of a picture.

It is the picture of an experiment that was made several hundred years ago by [the English mathematician and physicist] Isaac Newton, and, probably long before him, by other people to show how white light is connected with the seven colors.* When he made this experiment, Newton went into a dark room and let the sunlight in through a tiny little pinhole in the window. He then passed the narrow pencil of light that came through the hole through a triangular prism and discovered, as people had discovered long before him, that the white light was split up into the seven colors of the rainbow. I have made a drawing of this (Figure 4.1):

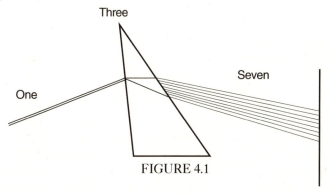

FIGURE 4.1

---

* c.f. *All and Everything*, p. 834, for a description of the apparatus Alla-Attapan, which is used to illustrate the universality of the Law of Sevenfoldness.

Until then, it was believed that the prism did something to the light, changed it. Newton discovered that the prism did not change the light and that it was possible by putting in a second prism, as is shown in the diagram below (Figure 4.2)—making a square instead of two triangles—to recombine the light that had been split up into the colors and to produce again a beam of white light.

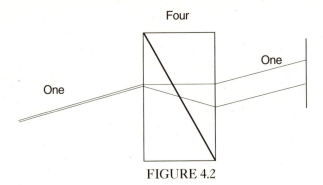

FIGURE 4.2

There is a small but important change, and that is that the source of light appears to be a little nearer, as we can see, for example, when we look obliquely through water into a pool, which makes the bottom of the pool seem a little nearer.

Now if I ask, what have we been talking about, how would you answer? Would you say we have been talking about the properties of light, about the white ray, or would you say that we have been talking about the colors that would be thrown on the screen or talking about the prism and crystal and what a crystal does to light that passes through it? You would say that we have been talking about all of these, not one of them in particular but about the whole experiment. This is the first thing that I want you to see from this picture that I have put in front of you. There is a whole situation to be talked about, and this is true also when we talk about man.

We want to talk this evening about individuality, about man's "I," the "I" that is in a real man. You remember the passage that I quoted at the beginning of this lecture, "The difference between what is called that 'I' which should be in the common presence of a real man and the pseudo 'I' which people to-day mistake for it." I want to draw your attention specially to the phrase *common presence* used in that extract, for it appears very often in Gurdjieff's writings.* When I said that we were speaking here about the whole experiment—the whole situation in which the white light, the prism, the colors, and the screen onto which they are thrown are combined—I could have said that we were speaking about the "common presence" of the experiment, all the different elements that go to make it up, elements quite different in their nature but all of which together make up the common presence of an experiment; in the same way, Gurdjieff talks about the common presence of a man. He also talks about the common

* c.f. *All and Everything*, p.1190–1,

presence of a planet, the common presence of the earth. This is a very useful phrase because it saves us from the mistake of talking about one part of the man as if it were the whole man; of talking, for example, about what we see, his body and its manifestations, as if they were the whole man; or what he experiences, his own thoughts and feelings and joys and sufferings, as if they were the whole of him; or, in the way we spoke last week [*see* chapter 3], about the man that belongs to the world of facts and the man that belongs to the world of possibilities, as if one or the other of those were *the* man, whereas it is both of them that make his common presence.

Now let us look for that part of the common presence of man that should be his "I". Maybe when you looked at this picture on the board, you thought ,"Ah, he is talking about the real 'I' and the false 'I.' Probably the picture at the top, where the single prism breaks the white ray up into the seven colors, corresponds to the false or illusory 'I' in man, and the one that stands foursquare at the bottom, which is able to transmit the white ray without breaking it up, corresponds to the real man, the real 'I'." Unfortunately, that is going a little too fast. Neither of these drawings here represents man as we know him. There is another more familiar arrangement than this that corresponds to man as we know him. It is the working of a cinema projector.

If we go to a cinema, we see a "world" thrown onto the screen: people in action with all their usual surroundings. This is done by an arrangement rather like that which we have been looking at, in which a ray of white light is intercepted on the way to the screen, but with the difference that, in place of the prism, there is a film. On the film, there are pictures, colored or uncolored, that intercept and absorb some of the light, leaving the remainder only to pass through onto the screen. There is a part of man as we know him that corresponds to the film, which changes the white light on its way to the screen.

When a child is born, it has something like a clean film, through which light can pass without distortion or change: it is not split into the seven colors nor recombined. The light passes out again through the transparent film as pure as when it enters. Then we proceed in that child to put all sorts of things on to the film: figures, colors, scenery, and so on. This process is what we call "education."* What is put on the film is not the child's own but what he gets from us and from all his experience of the world. Thereafter, when the white light passes through, it begins to throw images on the screen. The colors and shapes on the film are what we call the "personality" of the child, and the more varied and complicated and ingenious these shapes are, the more we say "This is a well-educated, civilized person."

This arrangement does not mean that the other has disappeared or been destroyed. The other arrangement, consisting of the prism and the light that goes to the screen in pure colors, corresponds to the real nature of the man, which Gurdjieff calls his "essence." The prism is the way into the world of possibilities, but light is reflected at its surface and is turned back into the world of facts. Something is done to the surface of the prism that prevents the light from

---

* c.f. *All and Everything*, p.1208,

passing through it, and little by little, the child ceases to know that there is a world of possibilities and thereafter lives entirely or almost entirely in the world of facts—that is, his personality.

The common presence of men such as we know them consists of the cinema film arrangement, the personality, in full operation, and the other part of the apparatus, the essence, put away, as it were, in a cupboard and ignored.

Last week, in reply to a question, I said that a child probably sees colors and shapes more nearly as they really are; that is, a hundred times more vividly and significantly than we do. That would correspond to the light that goes directly through the prism. In the world of facts, a great part of the light is absorbed by the coloring matters in the film, and, what is much worse, we are able to see only the previously prepared images; that is to say, we can experience nothing that does not come from the pictures already prepared for us in childhood. The cinematograph apparatus [that is, the projector] is arranged in such a way that the images are constantly being shuffled and reshuffled. This we call "living." It is all our automatic reaction to our environment, all our mechanical activity, and we scarcely know anything but this cinema show.

This does not mean that the other world—that of possibilities—has ceased to exist. It is always there, and some part of our common presence touches its frontier, only we never enter it, but turn back into the world of facts. Nevertheless, although we, in our ordinary consciousness, do not enter it, it acts upon us and arouses in us dissatisfaction with the life of fact alone and with it the need to find our own real being. Since, however, we have no idea of what it means to be our real selves or how to enter that world, we invent a substitute for our real self. We say "I" all the time, but in doing so, we refer only to our transient experience of the images thrown onto the screen by the light distorted, absorbed, and adulterated as it passes through us. The belief that I am this cinema show of images is a great illusion, and it prevents us from finding what we really are. To that half-read world belong not only our daydreams but all that we call living and doing—for these are merely automatic reactions of the same stuff as dreams are made of—while the real world, with its limitless possibilities, remains beside us, unnoticed and untried.

Now let us return to the first diagram (*see* Figure 4.1) and ask ourselves how a man can become such that he is able to transmit, without distorting it, the light that passes through him. For this, first of all, the surface of the prism must be cleaned so that the light can enter instead of being reflected back through the cinema film. That cleaning of the surface is accomplished through self-knowledge, by learning to recognize the difference between what is really ours and what is only borrowed from outside us.

After that, it is necessary for the prism itself, which exists in us only as a possibility, to be "crystallized." You may have noticed that I put in the first diagram the numbers one, three and seven (*see* Figure 4.1). I did this because in the common presence of a real man, three laws govern and hold everything together. One is the Law of Unity—that is represented here by the uniqueness of the white light—that is always the same everywhere. Another is the Law of

Threefoldness, which is represented by the triangular prism, that has the proper-ty of dividing the white light, enabling it to appear in another aspect of its nature; that is, an aspect of its nature in which it is not one but seven, the seven fundamental colors. This stands for the Law of Sevenfoldness or the law of octaves, as Gurdjieff calls it.

The relationship of one, three, and seven belongs to the structure of the real world, where man can be himself. We have, however, to understand that the light—the white light that is one—does not come from the man himself. We might say that it comes from beyond him, from the sun, and is present always. Also, the world of facts into which man enters, and in which he must participate, is not himself either. Man cannot be without the light, and he cannot exist with-out the world, but his role is to stand between the two and to be a link connect-ing the one with the other.

The triangle in Figure 4.1 stands for something that can be formed in man as a result of his own efforts, his own striving. It comes from the process that I have spoken of in each of these lectures, that is, the struggle of "yes" and "no." By this struggle something opens in man and, little by little, allows the light pene-trating into his common presence to collect into little pools that gradually merge into one another and crystallize. This crystal then can become the single prism that can receive the light and transmit it in the form of "essence experience" without distortion or change.

You may remember that I spoke last week [*see* chapter 3] about the work of attention and said that through attention we are able to stand between the world of facts and the world of possibilities. We can say now that, interpreted in terms of this picture, the white light comes from the world of possibilities, the images on the screen are the world of facts, and our attention is that which is able to meet the light and determine the form that it will have when it appears on the screen. We can learn to use our attention in such a way that we are sensitive both to the world of facts and to the world of possibilities, and that double sensitive-ness will enable us both to look toward the source, whence the light comes, and to look toward the screen, where the world of facts is unrolling itself, and to adjust the needs of the one to the needs of the other.

That is the wonderful power that attention has when it is developed and rightly used. Gradually, there can be formed in the common presence of a man something that can be called the body of his consciousness. That body of his consciousness corresponds to the prism that is there in Figure 4.1. This is called by Gurdjieff in *All and Everything* the *kesdjan* body or second body of man.* It is that through which he has the power to transmit consciously the light that enters him from beyond himself and to let it pass into the world of facts without losing its own natural colors. It does not mean that this second or "consciousness body" of man is always so flawless, so clean that it does not distort in some way the light that is passing through it.

The two parts of our cinema apparatus—the one that corresponds to the film

---

* c.f. *All and Everything*, p.764,

and the one that corresponds to the prism—are only separate and able to work quite independently in a man who has developed in a fully normal, one can even say in an ideal, way. Both film and prism have to be there. The formation of the second does not mean that the first can be dispensed with because it also has to play its part. Because of that, it is very difficult to prevent the one from having some effect upon the other.

To put it without any metaphor, I can say this—that in the automatic formation of man from childhood, there comes into existence his personality, which is the sum of all that he has learned, all his experiences, all his habits, and so on, through which he reacts to the world. That personality is an automatically acting mechanism. It has no initiative. It must always be passive. What is worse, it cannot help impressing its own images on the consciousness that is transmitted through it. At the same time, it is an indispensable instrument because it is the means by which man adapts himself to the conditions of the world in which he lives. I have spoken disparagingly about education and about the harm that we do to our children by putting a very unbalanced and unsatisfactory lot of images onto that clean film with which they are born. But that does not mean that there is any way out of it. At best, we can only hope not to spoil too much and not to prepare a situation that makes the subsequent formation of the real permanent instrument too difficult or even impossible because, for the purposes of adaptation to life, we need that sort of mechanism, the mechanism of personality. The other—the real permanent instrument—can be called the instrument of the essence. It is that which belongs to the real nature of man—"real" in the sense of belonging to his world of possibilities, that is, not destroyed by time. However, you must understand that the formation of that instrument does not proceed automatically, as does the formation of the mechanism of personality. It is possible only through our own efforts. It has to be paid for. Unless it is earned, we cannot have it because it is of such a nature that it is our very own, and nothing can be our very own unless we have earned it. When that is formed in man, he can truly say "I" because there is a point at which his consciousness is able to stand free and independent between the two worlds.

He then becomes a being not of two but of three worlds. There is first the world of pure consciousness, the world from which the white light comes. There is, secondly, the world of facts, where all the colored images appear on the screen; but, thirdly, there is also man's own world, the world where he is able to be himself. Yet still something is missing because all that he is able to do so far is to transmit the light undistorted in one direction. He is able to give something to the world of facts, but he is not by this able to return anything to the other world. For that, another part has to be formed that corresponds to the second prism, that seen in Figure 4.2. That is what Gurdjieff calls the Higher Being Body of man or, sometimes also, his soul.* Only when that third part is formed can the light pass through him in both directions, and then also he has that special property about which I spoke earlier, that the source of light appears to him as a little

---

* c.f. *All and Everything,* p. 765 and pp. 1124–5.,

nearer. The light that passes through him then, and falls on the world of facts, has been brought a little nearer through having passed through him. That is something he is able to do because he has become such that he has in him both of the two higher parts. Not only that, but he no longer is restricted to one direction. The difference between the man in Figure 4.1 and the man in Figure 4.2 is that the former is able to respond to the light but cannot reenter it, for in order to enter it, he has to have both of the higher parts formed in him, whereas the man in the latter can both respond to and also reenter into the light.

Now with the help of these figures, maybe it will be easier to follow what I am going to say about individuality, the real "I" that should be in a man, and about that which we call "I" in people such as we know. Calling by the name of "I" some part of our common presences that has no right to the name is one of the great harms that we do to ourselves, and it is, moreover, a great harm that we encourage in one another. None of us is ourself or able to be ourself. We are merely cinematograph films, transmitting the accidentally formed images of the past, reshuffled by the changing influences of life; and we call that film "I." Whenever we say "I think," "I feel," "I know," "I do," and so on, we are only saying it about that cinematograph film, but you must remember that that cinematograph film did not come from us. It is not really our own. It came to us from all the things that are outside us, from childhood onward. There is nothing that we think or say, no beliefs, no opinions, no ways of acting, or anything else, that is our own. All of it has come to us by the action of our environment, by what we call education and the whole process of life. We make a great mistake in calling all that "I".

This mistake that we all make matters very much because it prevents us from looking to the place where "I" really is; that is, the place where something can be formed in me that is able consciously and intentionally to perform this task of transmitting the light that enters me. If we wish to find the real world, one of the first things we have to do is to learn how to examine ourselves and see—really see—that all that we are accustomed to call "I" in ourselves is not "I" at all, and could not be. "I" cannot be my thoughts nor anything that is in my thoughts. "I" cannot be my feelings, my likes, my dislikes, nor any of my subjective reactions. I cannot be my body and all its appetites and the rest, as I tried to show you in one of the earlier lectures, but it is not enough that I should agree to that as a plausible argument. I must discover it in my own experience. I must come to the point where I see for myself that all these are not "I" and that I am not at all entitled to say "I" about anything that I notice in myself. Only then will I be able to begin to look for the place where "I" really is.

There are ways of making that search, that we need to learn. When we find that place, we can also learn how to bring to it that which should be there; that is, a crystal able to transmit light but, at the same time, able to divide all its colors and direct each of them into its own place. The formation of that crystal in us, that prism, which I called the "consciousness body," is one great part of the work by which man is able to become himself. The second great part, which corresponds to the formation of the second prism, requires a different kind of payment about which I have to speak specially in our lecture next week (*see* Chapter 5). However, there is one more interesting idea that we can get while keeping to this picture that I have spoken of tonight. I have spoken all along about the white light that comes from the sun, as if it were itself indivisible or, rather, homogeneous, but we know that in the light that comes from the sun, there is hidden a pattern, a pattern that cannot be discovered just by a simple experiment like this one with a prism, which will only show how it is divided into the seven primary colors. When a much more delicate experiment is carried out, such as was done by [the English chemist and physicist William Hyde] Wollaston and [the Bavarian optician Joseph von] Fraunhofer, finer lines appear in that rainbow—in that spectrum—and they have a pattern in them.

Now the remarkable thing is that the study of that pattern has told us all that we know about how the universe is made. We have no other knowledge about what the whole universe is made of, with the exception only of the surface of our own little earth, except through the study of this pattern, which is carried through the light of the sun and the stars. There is something just like that in the common presence of a man. Man has an instrument that is able to be sensitive to this pattern, and that really makes a fourth part of man, in addition to those about which I have spoken; this fourth part Gurdjieff calls Objective Reason. The way to it is what I spoke of last week [*see* Chapter 3]; that is, through Conscience. To be able to be sensitive to that pattern, which is present in all consciousness, that is the highest power that man is able to reach. This fourth part is a property of the completely transformed and developed man only, but I speak of it tonight so that we can have the whole picture before us and also so that those of you who have read, for example, P.D. Ouspensky's *In Search of the Miraculous*, (1949) can understand why I have spoken about three bodies, whereas he speaks about four.

Objective Reason is that part of man through which he becomes a vehicle of the Will. You remember that I spoke about three aspects of everything that exists: the aspect of Function, the aspect of Consciousness, and the aspect of Will, and I said will is the pattern in which the whole reason of everything that exists is contained. The reason why we have to leave the study of will, why I can say no more than to indicate its place, is just that: that so far as all ordinary experience of man is concerned, the distinctions of will really play no part. It is already a very big thing if man is able to come to what is shown here in Figures 4.1 and 4.2, that is, to be one through whom the will is able to be transmitted without distortion, but to discern the pattern itself—to be able consciously to play a part in the working out of the whole scheme of reality—belongs only to the highest possible development. It does not mean, of course, that will plays no part in the life of ordinary man. Will enters into everything. This could be expressed by changing the analogy we have taken that compares consciousness to light and say that will is like electricity, and think of everything in the world as worked by electrical forces, as, on the whole, it is. We would say that only very specialized instruments could do anything with the inner character of electricity, and while, for the most part, electrical instruments do depend just upon polarity—the presence of positive and negative electricity—there are some special instruments that are able to discover and respond to something deeper in the inner structure of electricity; strangely enough, these instruments are just beginning to be discovered today by our own sciences.

The analogy that compares electricity and will is not my own. It is used all through Gurdjieff's book, *All and Everything,* where he speaks of the omnipresent *okidanokh,** by which everything is moved, and of the possibility of dividing it into its constituent parts. Will is the pattern that the whole universe exists to realize, and, at the same time, it is the force that makes its realization possible. You see from what I am saying that it is only a man in whom all this has been developed—in whom all this has come to life—that can be spoken of as an Individual in the true sense of the word because it is only a fully conscious being who is able to see the pattern for himself. Only such a being is free, and hence Gurdjieff says that Will is the prerogative only of the highest level of man. However, individuality has gradations. In each one of us—such as we are now today—there is a possibility of individual existence. Our tragedy is that we forget that it is a possibility and not a fact, and we are content to put up with a substitute that is little more than a mere name: the "I-in-quotation-marks" of which Gurdjieff speaks.** This saves us the trouble of searching for the way to the real I—but what does it mean not to search? It means to abandon all that is truly significant in human life and to be content to remain as a mere apparatus for transforming energy.

QUESTIONS AND ANSWERS

Question: I cannot see how, if our personality is just a cinematographic screen, all of us can respond differently to the same stimulus, as, for instance, tonight all of us have listened with great interest to your lecture, but I am convinced there are very many of us who have responded entirely differently, which seems to me to be due to the mental mechanism—if you like, that film—your words must pass through before they reach the personality. First of all, to achieve that soul of superhuman being that we aim at, we have to use the best manifestations of our organism, which Gurdjieff rejects as automatic. But I do not see how we can ever achieve objectively that higher superbeing if we have to use means that he condemns as mere physical automatic means, seeing that it is only a soul of superhuman being that enables us to transcend all the manifestations of our organism.

J.G. Bennett: There are two separate questions. I think I had better tell the truth. I have already forgotten what the first one was.

Q.: Why do we react differently? How is it that we all react differently if we are nothing but cinematograph films?

J.G.B.: That is very simple. Each film is filled up with different material— we have different habits, different points of view, different words, and different meanings that we attach to words. Therefore, five hundred people here tonight,

---

* c.f. *All and Everything,* p.138,
** c.f. *All and Everything,* p. 1191.

all hearing even the same word, pronounced in the same tone of voice, will understand it in five hundred different ways. That is inevitable. Even though I have tried to avoid bringing into play your automatic associations with words, and speak with the help of pictures, I know that still we all of us inevitably react with the material that we have, that is, the material that is on our various films. You said the film "interposed" between the hearing and our personality, but the film *is* our personality. There is not something else behind all these habits of thought, all these acquired reactions. They are our personality, and all our experiences pass through that film. We talk as if there were an "I" behind it all—as if "I" think, "I" agree, "I" disagree, "I" like what you say, "I" dislike it, "I" find it interesting, "I" find it dull. But it is not like that. *It* thinks, *it* likes, *it* finds it dull; *it* in each case being that film which is all the time unwinding in front of the light. Of course the content of that film is different for each person, and therefore each person has a different reaction.

Now about the second part of the question, which is really this: How can an automatic mechanism, of the sort that I have just been describing, produce something that is nonautomatic, free, and conscious? It cannot, and it is not from our personality that this is produced. The formation of the vehicle of the "I" corresponding to the first prism in the picture is not just a transformation of personality. Personality does not turn into something different. As I said during the lecture, it always remains what it is, and it has its own part in our common presence.

That which is able to be "I" is independently formed by a different process, that is, by the struggle of "yes" and "no" made possible through our power of attention. The struggle of "yes" and "no" means to direct my attention here rather than there, and it is possible in me and in all of us because we have in our common presence both an affirming and a denying part. My personality is the instrument of my denying part. The possibility of "I" is the instrument of my affirming part, and although it is only a possibility, nevertheless, as I said last week, it *is*, and it has power, and thus there can be set up in me a struggle between possibility and fact. So that it is not that the lower is transformed into the higher or that the higher itself comes into existence spontaneously but that something between the two arises as the result of the struggle between them. That is the principle of the Law of Threefoldness that I mentioned in the lecture and why I put the number three over the prism in the middle [*see* Figure 4.1]. Out of the struggle of yes with no, of affirmation with denial, comes a third force, which is consciousness, that gives the possibility of "I." That is why I said that I am neither the light nor yet am I the image on the screen, but if *I am*, then I am the crystal through which the light passes, and something is added as it passes through.

So you see that question—How is it that out of the automatism something can arise?—is answered in this way: The automatism, the passive, denying part, is indispensable to the process, but the process itself could not move unless there were something also that could say "yes." That something is present in us very intermittently, only at moments—as I said last week—and what happens to us depends upon the use that we make of those moments.

Another analogy that Gurdjieff was fond of using compared that personality—that automatism—to the soil, in which a seed is planted. The seed has to take its nourishment from the soil. It withdraws something from it for its own life, and without the soil, it cannot grow. However, the soil itself is not transformed. The soil remains.

Q.: If a man's personality has nothing to do with his essence or his soul, why are some personalities admirable and lovable and others repellent?

J.G.B.: There is something in the quality of the material of which the film is made that we can call the hereditary factor. There is also something in the conditions of early life. By the combination of these, and other factors as well, the resulting film may be, as you say, more lovable and attractive or more repellent. That is not quite the whole story because I said that there must be some interaction between the two. Man is not wholly his personality. His common presence includes also his possibilities, and they have some effect also. In all more or less normal people there is some interaction between the two worlds. It is an abnormal, spoiled person who is cut off entirely from the world of his possibilities. A very tragic situation that unfortunately does arise in life is where people become altogether identified with the world of facts and lose all contact with, all possibility of looking toward, the other world. Sometimes a man may gain all he wants in the world of facts, but the price he pays may be much too great. If he could see, if he could *really* see, what was happening to him, he would sooner die than remain like that, but it is just because he cannot see that he gives himself entirely to the world of facts.

Q.: Can it also be tragic for a person to live too much in this other world and to lose contact with the world of facts?

J.G.B.: Yes, of course, it can. Just as tragic. No, not just as tragic; but it also brings things to an end for him. Why is that? Because he lives in that other world only in his dreams. If he really lived in it, it would be different, but to live wholly in that world is possible only in dreams. If one is awake, one must be awake to both worlds, not to one only. It can happen, of course, that someone will turn away from the world of facts but not be ready to pay the price to live in both worlds. Then they simply go into a world of dreams, and then also they lose everything, only they lose it in a way that is a little different from the other—not so tragic but even more irreparable, for the first man can sometimes be saved by suffering whereas the second remains forever in his dreams.

Q.: In answering the question before the last, you said of a man who is cut off from his possibilities that if he sees the situation he will be made miserable by it and try to do something about it. What do you mean by "he"?

J.G.B.: There are degrees of "he-ness." It depends how deeply he is touched. It is possible for him to see something just with one of his centers, to know it only with his thinking part, or to experience it emotionally from some shock, for example, some personal loss or from seeing some disaster happening very close to him that shows what man's life is really like. Owing to the strong imitativeness of our physical organism, it can also happen that the stimulus can come just through the instinctive part alone. So it may happen that severe illness, or the severe illness of someone close or something like that, will wake up one part of us to the realization that we are not on firm ground. When this happens, something inwardly can open to that place in the common presence of a man of which I spoke last week, that is, his Conscience. Then he experiences a state called "remorse." Gurdjieff uses the term remorse in general for all that kind of experience that I have been describing, where through some event a man is obliged to see that he has nothing and is nothing. With that, there may arise in him an affirmation that he will do something about it. Unfortunately, we have a countermechanism in us, to which also Gurdjieff gives a name—that is, he calls it self-calming—by means of which we at once turn ourselves away from this experience of remorse, which is very painful for our personalities, and contrive to forget about it. So although it actually happens in the life of people that, much more frequently than one might suppose, they wake up to the real situation. Nevertheless, it does relatively little for them because of this property of self-calming. Sometimes it will happen that instead of having recourse to self-calming,* a man will try really to do something about it—something that will, in general, begin to open him to this whole process that we have been speaking about. Everything is possible for us just because this ableness to respond to the light is not dead in us, and so long as that ableness is not dead, everything remains possible. Still, a man can go through many years without even suspecting that such a problem exists for him, and then something will touch him and he will experience an effectual moment of remorse.

Q.: Do you think that it is never possible to waken in the manner you have just spoken of or to transcend oneself in the way you described before? The result of which is an intellectual process, being initiated by a violent emotional disturbance. You may discuss philosophy, people may follow your meaning, but unless they have suffered some emotional disturbance, they cannot grasp the full meaning of your words.

J.G.B.: The emotional realization that we are betraying our real destiny may come at the beginning or it may come later. You remember I said to you before that we are very, very different; we are different not only in our personalities but also in the form of our essence, that is, in the form of our will, about which I have really not been able to speak yet. Because of this, the way in which these things can open for us is very different, and every kind, every type of situation can have its chance. There are some people, for example, who, feeling nothing at all, can begin just by imitating someone else. I have seen people begin such work for no other reason than that they saw that somebody rather influential was interested in it and they thought they might get a boost out of it. They got caught. They ended up by having—I thought of one in particular—a worse emotional disturbance by coming to it later than if they had come to it at the beginning.

Q.: It is not merely an emotional disturbance is it? It is this that you were talking of before, the ability to shove away the pain?

J.G.B.: Yes. One can start from almost any motive. I have seen that in long

* c.f. *All and Everything*, pp. 105, 538, 609, 782, 954, 1059–60, 1126, 1144, 1211, and 1222-3.

years of experience with hundreds, probably thousands, of people. There is a very beautiful parable of Jeláluddin Rumi, the greatest of Moslem Sufi teachers, in which he speaks of a man who has lost a camel. The caravan is about to start and he realizes he has not got his camel and night is coming on. He gets frantic about it, runs here and there, asking everyone, "Have you seen such and such a camel looking like this or that?" They all begin to say, "Yes, I have seen such a camel, it has got lop ears, it has got bandy legs, or something of the sort." The man still runs about, looking for the camel, and another man sees him making all this fuss and notices all the attention he is attracting to himself. The second man begins to shout also, "I have lost a camel" and he also begins asking, "Where's my camel?" just simply out of imitation and because he sees that this other man is getting after something. Finally, after a great deal of suffering, the first man— the true camel seeker—finds his camel, but then the surprising thing is that the other also finds a camel. Then the second man says to the first, "Because you had lost a camel, you sought but because I sought, I found I had lost a camel."

Q.: Do we have to work through all the out-of-date, secondhand reactions that we have collected in our minds or may we in some other way put those on one side? Is that a process of escaping or do we have to meet the old material day by day, hour by hour, minute by minute?

J.G.B.: What are we to do? I think I spoke about Gurdjieff's analogy, didn't I, of the house with four rooms? It is also very interesting. I will tell you his story of the house with four rooms—that man has a house with four rooms. He only lives in one room, and that is filled with rubbish so that he can hardly move around. Then he accidentally finds that all that matters to him is in the fourth room, which he has never entered. In order to get into the fourth room, he has to pass through the other three. The first room is this room of his personality. The second room is the room in which his essential nature is. The third room is the room of the "I"? It is only in the fourth room, where there is Objective Reason, that he will find what he is really looking for. However, he cannot hope to get into the second room, which leads out of the first, so long as the first is so full of rubbish. Certainly, he has to do some tidying. But what is important is that if he goes through that process, step-by-step, when he gets to the fourth room he will find what he wants there. It will all have been prepared, although he did not know it. There are illegitimate ways. There are ways by which one can get to the fourth room without having done all that tidying work and without having gone step-by-step through it all, but then, if one gets to the fourth room that way, one will find it empty and it is too late to put anything there. So what you say about having to face all that we have—we must do so. Much has to be done. For example, I have said several times this evening, and before, that I am not—and cannot be—either my functions or any part of them. To discover that this is so for one-self is to see what it means; to experience this, beyond all possibility of any doubt, itself tidies everything up in the first room to an extraordinary degree. Then it is really possible to pass through to, and begin to work in, the second room; only it is not sufficient just to think that it is so. One has to experience this oneself. As soon as you begin to experience this, you begin to find one tidy place in yourself—one place where you can have a bit of peace and where you are not compelled to live all the time with lies and nonsense. That in itself is worth a good price.

Q.: If we take a child and a teacher, and the teacher is trying to see the possibilities of the child, what is the process? How can she understand—can she realize—those possibilities and be able to keep the screen of the child's personality as simple and pure as possible?

J.G.B.: The question is one I am asked more often than any other, and rightly so, because it is the key to the future. First of all, no one can see the possibilities of another. We must know that, when we are in front of a child, we are in front of a being whom we cannot know. If we try to begin knowing that being, already we are off onto personality. What I must remember—and that is itself a real discipline for me—is that this is an unknown being and that it is the unknown possibilities of that being that matter—not the facts that I am inevitably putting into that child. I must bring that in myself, by keeping present in me this memory that it is the invisible child that matters far more than the visible one, and also accepting that I am not able to see that invisible child—any more than anyone else can—because invisible does not mean just around the corner; invisible means belonging to a different world. I advise you, if you deal with children, to try the simple experiment of not letting yourself, when in front of the child, think What are the possibilities? What can this child become? but simply to remember that this is a being who has possibilities that no one can know. In other words, remember the invisible child as you look at the visible one. You have to see and to deal with the visible child. That is inevitable. Still remember the other, and do not try to know it, because if you try to know it, you are merely bringing yourself back into the realm of fact.

If you will keep that discipline with yourself, you will see that, so long as you keep it, something will be different in your relation with the child. Something will pass from you to the child that is more necessary to him than what you are able to give in the world of facts, and it will have the effect that the two will be able to be harmonized. You have, in any case, to transmit material of personality, but you will also be transmitting material of essence. Only one thing I say once again, don't let yourself think what the possibilities actually consist of. That is what people find very hard. They cannot help speculating what this child might be—What will he be?—instead of keeping only in front of them that there is that invisible child there also.

Q.: Should one apply that to adults also?

J.G.B.: What is behind "should"? For what? If you wish their true welfare, then the answer is "yes." If I wish the true welfare of another person, I must, in looking at that person, remember that his common presence is composed not only of what I see but also of what I do not see. If I remember that, I will be able to wish his welfare more or less as I ought to—more or less as it is necessary for him.

Q.: When one has reached the stage of accepting, believing and understanding all that you have told us tonight, is it not inevitable that one would automatically lose self-confidence and all optimism? If so, is not the next step to fall either into a floating existence where one does nothing and cares nothing or, worse still, into the depths of despair and frustration? What alternatives have you to offer us for two of the most essential parts of man's makeup—self-confidence and optimism?

J.G.B.: There is false self-confidence and false optimism and there is true. I cannot imagine—I really cannot imagine—a more optimistic picture than I have put before you this evening. I have spoken about a really limitless possibility of transformation for man, of the attainment of something that ordinarily he cannot even dream about; and, moreover, of that as something that is open to all of us and that does not require any special kind of preparation or fortunate conditions. But there is—you know what I said to the other lady who spoke about rubbish— a great deal of rubbish that has to be dealt with, but if someone goes into a room that is full of rubbish, is it pessimism to face the fact that it is rubbish and that there is some cleaning up to be done?

Also, you must remember that the start is very simple indeed; the start is to recognize what I can do, and what I can do is to choose yes or no in relation to the way that I allow my energies to flow.

Now about self-confidence. Truly people have not got self-confidence. When you say that self-confidence is one of the most important attributes for man, you are quite right. It is really an important thing. Man must have it. But how do people really exist? They have a deep-seated fear and lack of self-confidence hidden by superficial activity. What they call self-confidence—what they call being successful and well-adapted people—is simply the extent to which they have a good mechanism for self-calming—a good means for hiding from themselves their own nothingness. If you really could see how people are—why everyone is a slave, why everyone is so dependent upon the opinion of others, why, always, all people require in some way bolstering up—then you would understand that, at bottom, nobody faces the fact that they have no "I" and that, therefore, as I said earlier this evening, they have to live with a false "I"—with an affirmation of something that is not there. That affirmation is so precarious that they have to spend nearly all their energy in bolstering it up and in persuading other people to bolster it up. When they see, then they do not fear any more because they also see that there is something to be done. I say this—that only one man is truly without fear, that is, the man who works on himself and knows that he is doing whatever is in his power to accomplish the task that is in front of him. Everyone else is afraid. But why should you think that this study engenders pessimism or lack of courage? It is not so.

Q.: Could you say something about heredity?

J.G.B.: Yes. About one-third of our possibilities come to us from our parents and, with them, about one-third of our disabilities. We have in the spiritual sense a certain pattern, and also a certain debt, that is derived from the way our parents lived—and our grandparents and great-grandparents and so on. We cannot dissociate ourselves from them, not all our possibilities and disabilities—I said about one-third each because there are other factors that are equally important and that have nothing to do with heredity. You can see in children—in a number of children of the same family—that certain things clearly are the result of heredity and that other things are quite independent of it. If there is anything more you want to know about it, tell me, but a whole lecture on heredity would require an evening given to it.

Q.: Is this process of self-realization or greater awareness—they might not be the right words—is that process conducive to real happiness?

J.G.B.: You must know what are the laws of happiness. There cannot be happiness without suffering. There is no such thing as free happiness. Happiness has to be paid for. There is only one difference: one can pay for it in advance or one can pay for it in arrears. Clever people pay first and are happy afterward. It is really so. You just ask yourself that question: Can there be even any meaning in the idea of unearned happiness? Can you picture to yourself that happiness that was not paid for could have any reality? It is one of the kinds of questions that one must put to oneself and oblige oneself to face. It is through not facing such questions as that that we live in such an illusory dreamworld. But if you ask me if this work is conducive to greater happiness, then I say yes because the whole of this work could be described as learning how to pay in advance and not in arrears.

"The striving from the beginning of their existence to pay for their arising and their individuality as quickly as possible, in order afterward to be free to lighten as much as possible the Sorrow of Our Common Father."

—*All and Everything*

Chapter 5

The Debt of Our Existence

Lecture 5: April 5, 1954

THE TITLE of tonight's lecture, "The Debt of Our Existence.," produces a revolt in some people. They find it difficult to accept that, by reason of our existence alone, we are placed under an obligation. I have heard people say lightheartedly, "I did not ask to be born. Have I not the right to be happy?" That kind of talk is stupid and blasphemous, and it is very noticeable that it does not come from people who really suffer but from those who are filled with imaginary fears and imaginary sufferings and who expect something from life that they themselves will not even take the trouble to earn.

We have to remember the situation in which we are and about which I spoke in the first of these lectures; that is, that undoubtedly we exist here on earth for a reason that is unconnected with our own personal likes and dislikes—our pleasure and displeasure—and that is part of the whole Universal Process of Reciprocal Maintenance, which we have to serve, whether it is pleasant to us or not. We should put ourselves in the position of our own animals. If I have a horse, I expect it to serve me—to draw the plow or the cart or to carry me if I wish to go on a journey—and I do not allow the horse to raise the question of its own right to be consulted as to whether or not it will consent to serve me for what I need. Certainly, when my horse has served me, I must not only look after its needs of food and shelter but I must treat it well. However, that comes after the service, and is not a bargain made before the service is given. We men and women must accept that we are in the same position.

Tonight I want to speak to you about the debt of our existence, and it requires to be thought of in three successive stages. The first stage refers to the condition that must be fulfilled before we can even begin to pay; the second is the debt itself and its payment; and the third is the situation of the man who has paid his debt and is free to do what he will.

It happens that this subject has been most wonderfully treated in a passage that I am going to take as the foundation of our talk this evening. It is chapter 25 of Saint Matthew's Gospel. This Gospel was compiled fifty or sixty years after the death of Christ by the school in North Syria that was no doubt closest to his teachings. It was constructed by people of great understanding. For forty years, I have studied it almost every day, and I have never failed to find something new. Chapter 25 contains the very last of Christ's teaching before the Passion. It is the

climax of the whole teaching—his last parables—and we must therefore take it
seriously indeed. When we examine it closely, we can see that there have been
placed in it secrets that enable us to understand the debt of our existence. You
no doubt remember in general these parables, but because it is necessary to
attend to details, I will repeat them to you.

The first is the parable of the wise and foolish virgins: "For the Kingdom of
Heaven shall be likened unto ten virgins that took their lamps and went forth to
meet the bridegroom. And five of them were wise, and five were foolish. And
they that were foolish took their lamps, but took no oil in their lamps. But the
wise took oil in their vessels with their lamps. And while the bridegroom tarried
they all slumbered and slept. And at midnight a cry arose, 'Behold the bridegroom cometh, go ye out to meet him.' And all those virgins arose and trimmed
their lamps. And those that were foolish said unto the wise, 'Give us of your oil,
for our lamps are going out.' But the wise answered and said unto them, 'It may
not be, for there will not be enough for us and for you. But go rather unto them
that sell and buy for yourselves.' And when they had gone out to buy, the bridegroom came, and those that were ready went in to the marriage and the door was
shut. And afterward there came the other virgins also, saying, 'Lord, Lord, open
to us.' But he answered and said unto them, 'Verily I say unto you, I know you
not.' Be awake,* therefore, for ye know neither the day nor the hour when the
Son of Man cometh."

That is the first of the three parts of that chapter. It applies to everyone, as is
shown by the number ten, which is the number of completeness. Therefore, it is
not a teaching intended only for some and not for others. Moreover, you will
understand that here the oil stands for energy. It is both a food and a source of
light. The virgins were obliged to have that oil as a condition of being able to
participate in the marriage. What most people do not notice in this parable is that
all the virgins had to obtain the oil. Even the foolish virgins had to go out and
buy the oil, although it was too late. They had to obtain the oil, even though it
could no longer give them admission to the bride chamber.

To understand this passage, we have to turn to *All and Everything*, especially
to chapter 48, "The Addition," where it is said that we all have to serve a very
great purpose and from this there is no escape for anyone. But it is possible to
serve this purpose wisely—consciously accepting the obligation—or to serve it
automatically, mechanically and unintentionally, in which case nothing is
received by the person who serves it. He serves—as Gurdjieff says—exclusively
only as a thing, which when no longer needed disappears forever. We have to
remember that all of us, without exception, have to produce that energy, either
in the process of our lives or in the process of our death. If we produce it in the
process of our lives, we are like the wise virgins, who are ready and are able to go
into the bride chamber. If not, we have to produce it when it is already too late
for us, that is, in our own death.

About what that means I will speak in the last lecture [*see* Chapter 6], but

---

* The Greek word *grigoreite* comes from egeiro, to wake up, to rouse or stir, and it can also
mean to rouse from the dead. Christ was called the grigoron phos—the awakened light.

before we leave this parable, I want to say a little more about the way in which this oil is bought. I said that it applies to us all—to all people—and that this is shown by the number ten of the virgins. All of us—all mankind—are in front of a certain visible demand, that is, the general demand of right action—what is called in Buddhism the *Silas** or, in the Christian teaching, the Law. You remember how the teaching of Christ begins with a warning that nothing that he will teach sets aside the obligation to fulfill the law. There is the nature of man with, at the bottom of it, a negative force—a denying force—from which comes our egoism, our self-love, and opposed to this denying force there is, before all people, a certain standard—certain rules. At all times, this standard and these rules have existed; they can be called the general moral sense of mankind. Between these two forces, that is, the forces of our own animal nature with the negative impulses that are involved in it and the requirements of the general morality of mankind, there must be a struggle. It is the primary struggle of "yes" and "no" that is before everyone. If we will not accept this—if we identify ourselves with all the negative forces that work in us—then nothing is produced.

We go, as I said before, by the line of least resistance, maybe conventionally following the customs of our society and avoiding unpleasant situations but, in reality, doing nothing, in truth not struggling at all with the negative forces in ourselves, with the denying, weak sides of our nature. If we live like that, then when we end our lives, the transformation of energy required of us will not have been completed—but it will have to be completed. That is what the parable of the foolish virgins must bring home to us.

We have to understand also from this that it is not sufficient to appear to conform to the general moral sense of the world—to appear to live by such rules as "do to others as you would they should do to you"—because from appearances there is no transformation of energy. The struggle must be engaged, and we have to acknowledge that in our times, on the whole, people do not see it like that. They are content with what seems, with appearing to live a life that conforms to the general moral sense of the world. But inwardly and in reality, it is not like that. That is why this parable finishes up with the words *grigoreite*, "rouse yourselves, wake up." This does not refer to some time in the future. It points to our present situation and the need to watch for the moments when something is present in us that is able to choose. That entry into us of the possibility of choosing is the coming of the Son of Man, and none of us can say that this never happens to us.

However, we become lazy and indifferent and close ourselves to this possibility of choosing, putting off always to another time all the awkward moments of choice that come before us the whole time—every day. It is at those moments that we can make that decision of "yes" against "no" by which the omnipresent active element *okidanokh*** is transformed in us. You understand that now I speak about everyone.

---

*c.f. *Digha Nikaya,* translated by T.W. Rhys Davids, vol. 2, the *Brahmagala and Samanna Phala Suttantras* where *silas* or "rules of morality" are contrasted with *dharma* or debt of our existence.
** see above, page 61.

The second parable changes the theme from the oil to the talents.* "In the same way, a man traveling into a far country called unto him his own servants and delivered unto them his goods. And unto one he gave five talents, and to another two, and to another one. To every man according to his several abilities or force. And straightway went abroad. And he that received five talents went and worked on it. And made five more talents beside. And he also that received two gained two other talents. But he that received one went and digged in the earth and hid the silver of his master. And after a long time the lord of those servants cometh and reckoneth with them. And so he that had received five talents brought another five, and saith: 'Lord, thou deliveredst unto me five talents, behold I have gained unto them five more.' His lord said unto him, 'Well done, thou good and faithful servant. Thou hast been faithful over a few things, I will make thee ruler over many things. Enter thou into the joy of thy lord.' And also he that received two talents came and brought other two, and said: 'Lord, thou deliveredst unto me two talents, behold I have gained another two besides them.' And he said unto him 'Well done, thou good and faithful servant; thou hast been faithful over a few things, I will make thee ruler over many things. Enter thou into the joy of thy lord.' But he that had received one talent came and said: 'Lord, I knew thee that thou art an hard man, reaping where thou has not sown, and gathering where thou has not strawed; and I was afraid. And I took thy talent and hid it in the earth. Lo, here is that which is thine.' And his lord answered and said unto him: 'Thou wicked and slothful servant, thou knewest that I reap where I sowed not, and gather where I have not strawed. Thou shouldst therefore have taken my money to the exchangers, so that on my return I should have received my own with profit. Take therefore the talent from him and give it unto him which hath ten talents. For unto everyone that hath shall be given and he shall have abundance, but from him that hath not shall be taken away even that he hath, and cast ye the unprofitable servant into outer darkness, there shall be weeping and gnashing of teeth.'"

This parable takes the whole problem of the debt of our existence an important step forward. Here, as distinct from the virgins, each of whom had one lamp only, all are not equal. Each receives according to his several abilities. What are the talents? The whole parable emphasizes that they are not the property—not the possession—of the servants but are a trust. Yet he who uses the five rightly and makes the other five is given all ten as his own property. The talents that are given from above, from the master to the servants, are the pattern of our possibilities. They are what we can make of our lives. They belong to the world of possibilities. They are not fact; they are not actual. What will become of them will depend upon what we do. Also, we have to understand that the work must be done in the absence of the master. He makes this arrangement and withdraws from the scene, and the servants are left to themselves—as it is with us in our own lives.

---

* This parable continues directly after the first without introduction. In the English translation, the words, "the Kingdom of Heaven is like unto" are inserted, but in the Greek, it goes on osartos, "in the same way."

There is in this parable an apparent injustice; that is, that the servant who receives one talent only, and who, according to the explanation, has less ability than the others, is penalized because he fails to use the relatively small possibility that is given to him. If you read the text carefully, particularly in the Greek—which probably must be the original language in which this Gospel was written—you see a difference between what is done by the first servant, who worked creatively, and the second, who worked to gain. The first stands for the man who is able to work creatively, who has such force in himself that he is able by his own work to accomplish the task that is in front of him. The number five stands for that level, that kind of possibility in man. The man with two talents gains through association with others. Both produce what is required of them and exactly the same words are spoken to the one as to the other. They both then enter into a different life where new possibilities open for them.

You should note very carefully what is said to the third servant. It is not said to him, "You should have worked creatively" or "You should have worked to gain" but "You should have taken your money to the exchangers." That means, "If you had not the force to do this by yourself, you should have put yourself into a relationship with others, through which this transformation could have taken place." All are equally called to account, the strong and the weak, but what is required of the strong and what is required of the weak are different; and they need one another for that reason. The weak servant knew, as all did, what was required of him, but he did not do what was possible for him, that is, join himself to others through whom his work would have been made fruitful.

So you see that in this parable of the talents, we have a more complete picture, a further stage, than is shown in the parable of the wise and foolish virgins. We enter the phase of *schoolwork*. We come to the summing up of all that Christ taught, from the moment at the outset of the Sermon on the Mount, when he said, "Except your righteousness exceed the righteousness of the scribes and Pharisees, ye shall in no wise enter the Kingdom of Heaven." From then until now, he taught this—that is, that something more is required than is represented by the parable of the wise and foolish virgins. There is required of us that we should accomplish what is possible for us. What the possibility is and how to accomplish it, we have to discover, either by ourselves or by going to those who are wiser than we are. Really, you must see that, just as the hidden key to the parable of the wise and foolish virgins is the compulsion on the virgins—both wise and foolish—to get the oil anyhow, so here it is the relationship of weak and strong and the answer to the question "And what about those who are too weak to work for themselves?" They can always join those who are stronger; by their joint endeavor, the task required of all can be accomplished.

We must note that the parable does not teach us the position of those who are strong enough to work yet do not work. Further, what is the meaning of the passage from Gurdjieff's book, [*All and Everything*] that I quoted at the beginning of this lecture; that is, "The striving from the beginning of their existence to pay for their arising and their individuality as quickly as possible, in order afterward to be free to lighten as much as possible the Sorrow of Our Common Father."

For this we have to turn to the third part of the chapter of Saint Matthew, and you must understand that all three parts are linked to the opening words of the chapter: "For the Kingdom of Heaven is like ..." The third part begins: "When the Son of Man shall come in his glory, and all the holy angels with him, and shall be seated on the throne of his glory, then shall all the nations be gathered unto him and he shall separate them as a shepherd divideth his sheep from his goats, and shall set the sheep upon the right hand and the goats upon the left. Then will he say unto them upon the right hand, 'Come, ye blessed of my father. Inherit the kingdom that is prepared for you from the foundation of the world. For I was anhungered and ye gave me meat, I was athirst and ye gave me drink, I was a stranger and ye took me in, naked and ye clothed me, sick, and ye visited me, in prison, and ye came unto me.' And then the righteous shall say unto him: 'Lord, when saw we thee anhungered and gave thee meat, or athirst and gave thee to drink, or a stranger and took thee in, or naked and clothed thee, or sick and in prison and came unto thee?' And then shall the King answer and say unto them, 'Inasmuch as ye did it unto the least of these my brethren ye did it unto me.' And then shall he say to them on the left hand, 'Depart from me ye cursed, into the fire of eternity that is prepared for the devil and his angels.* For I was anhungered and ye gave me not meat, athirst and ye gave me not drink, a stranger and ye took me not in, naked and ye clothed me not, sick and in prison, and ye came not unto me.' Then shall they answer and say unto him, 'Lord, when saw we thee anhungered or athirst, or a stranger, or naked, or sick and in prison, and ministered not unto thee?' And the King will answer and say unto them, 'Inasmuch as ye did it not unto the least of these, ye did it not unto me. These therefore shall go into the punishment of eternity, but the righteous into the life of eternity."

Each time the situation becomes more serious because now it speaks about people who have power to do something in the lives of their fellowmen and who therefore become involved in the world of possibilities. They do not remain outside in the world of facts, outside the door, as in the parable of the virgins, nor cast into darkness, as with the unprofitable servant, but they have to enter the fire of eternity, that is, the suffering of consciousness in the eternal world, the world of possibilities. They are what Gurdjieff calls *hasnamuss*,** and one must understand how their situation also arises. It refers to those who are strong and could work but either refuse or neglect to do so. The situation of the *hasnamuss* is altogether more serious because, as I said, he is already involved in that world—in the invisible world—and cannot escape.

The other side of this third part, or third parable—because, really, this is also a parable—concerns suffering. Here the King says, "Inasmuch as ye did it unto the least of these my brethren, ye did it unto me." We wrongly interpret that kind of saying as if it were vicarious kindness because we are so unaccustomed to thinking of the suffering of God and the needs of God that we do not under-

---

* The word *aionica* (angels) means that which has wings to eternity or the world of possibilities. It refers to the suffering of consciousness, as distinct from the suffering of body.
** c.f. *All and Everything*, page 203.

stand the most elementary truth; namely, that if God *is,* he must suffer all suffering. Thus, it is not the suffering of people but the suffering of God that is at stake. This is made as plain as it can be in this passage—perhaps as plain as the compilers of this Gospel dared to make it, having regard to the fact that it was a *legomonism,* that is, a means of transmitting to future time real secrets of the work.

There are one or two more things I wish to add to this. First of all, we can also call this the chapter about "I"? First there is "I" as the bridegroom—the "I" that enters as the active principle in relation to the passive. Then there is "I" as the master, who stands between the servants; and, thirdly, there is "I" as the King. There are three stages in the understanding and the experience of "I" that are presented in these three parables. Again, you must notice that the first parable refers to the virgins, that is, to women—the female principle—and the second to the servants, to men, that is, the active principle. That which is required in the first parable relates to the passive part. It is a universal passive principle out of which the energy must be transformed that is the oil of the lamps, and *must* be. In the second, it is the active principle that may or may not accomplish the task that is in front of it. Now, of course, you must not suppose that the parable of the virgins applies only to women, and the parable of the servants—of the talents—applies only to men. It is not so. In each of us, there is a passive and an active part, an affirmation and a denial. From each of these, something indispensable has to be brought forth in order to pay the debt of our existence. The debt is paid at the moment that the servant is able to come and say "Behold, I have made other five talents." But this is a task that stands over and above the indispensable obligatory work that belongs to the first part that is represented by the response of the virgins to the bridegroom.

Again, when we come to the third part of this chapter, we must not think of the world as divided into sheep and goats, righteous and sinners. It is a parable of the inner part of man. In each of us, there is the sheep and the goats, that is, that which affirms—which is on the side of work—and that which denies it. The coming of the Son of Man in this parable is the entry into us of that which is able to divide these two and keep them really separate in us, as the shepherd divides the sheep and the goats. We are accustomed to thinking of good as somehow existing by itself and of bad as existing by itself, without understanding that the two poles are necessary to one another—that affirmation cannot exist without denial and that there has to be in us a denying as well as an affirming principle. However, there also must enter into us—and this is really the whole meaning of our existence—yet another, a third principle, called here the Son of Man, which is able to keep them apart—for in the ordinary state of man, they are mixed, and every one of us must know, if we have any sincerity, that these in us are never separated. Always our affirmation is mixed and tainted with denials—always our denying part has something that justifies it. We cannot make that clean division that corresponds to the last verse of this chapter, "These therefore shall go into the punishment of eternity, but the righteous into the life of eternity." That is the great task for man: to be able to place in himself each where it should be and to keep them there. Only then does he become one who is able to do.

This brings us to the end of this explanation of the passage that I quoted in the syllabus. Reading this last parable superficially, one might suppose that doing good to others is a very simple matter—to feed the hungry, to take in the stranger, to clothe the naked. It is anything but so. The only way that we know how to clothe the naked is to take away somebody else's clothes. The only way that we know how to feed the hungry is to let somebody else starve. Because that is how our lives go. We are under such laws that whatever we do, we inevitably undo also because we are not free people. We have to learn to see, to recognize, that to feed the hungry or to clothe the naked is a supreme accomplishment, if it is to be done without betraying some other need. You may remember that, at one of the early lectures, someone spoke about responsibility toward others and said something equivalent to "What about feeding the hungry?" There is, of course, a feeding the hungry that belongs to the ordinary moral sense of mankind, but there are also other and deeper meanings that apply only to the man who is free, who is able to act so that his actions do not undo themselves. Such are the Elect, and, if we can find such people, it is to them that we must attach ourselves because they alone know how the hungry are to be fed. It is that feeding of the hungry that lightens the sorrows of Our Common Father, but we must not forget that it is the supreme achievement—the final significance of man's life—that he should be able to be a cause of a lightening of sorrow.* He is only free to become this after he has paid the debt of his own existence; for so long as he is in debt, the attempt to relieve hunger is a false charity, like one who is generous at the expense of his creditors or his family.

Each of these three parables represents one of what Gurdjieff calls the sacred impulses. The virgins live in hope. It is the hope of the bridegroom that enables them to go out and get the oil that is needed for their lamps. The servants work by faith. As the parable emphasizes, the master withdraws from the scene. Without his help and support, they have to accomplish their task. Those who have the power must work by love, as in the third part. What we have to understand, though, is that with us there is neither hope nor faith nor love. If any of us is able to be honest with himself or with herself, he or she must see that we are not able to accept anything that is written in this chapter and live by it. That is what is called in Gurdjieff's book, "The Terror of the Situation." That is why the only possibility for the regeneration of mankind is in the awakening of Conscience, which means light. Conscience is the power to see things as they are—to understand.

Always, man has been warned; all prophets, all great teachers have been warners. Always these things that I have been saying have been said, but people cannot or will not listen to them. In the Q'uran it is written: "Say; we did not destroy a city, but it had its warners to remind, and we are never unjust."** Every one of you, I expect, has read this chapter many times and other chapters of the Gospels or heard things; but which of us can say that we have been able to

---

* c.f. the doctrine of the Bodhisattva in Buddhism.
** c.f. Q'uran, chapter 26, verses 208 and 209.

listen to these warnings? If we know that we cannot, then we have to see that we must look for another way to the same end, but a way that is possible for us such as we are. Very much about this is certainly taught in these parables, but not how it is to be done. We read the words, "Wake up, for ye know neither the day nor the hour when the son of man cometh," and, in truth, we must acknowledge that they mean nothing to us, because we do not even know how to wake up.

And yet, which of us can say that it is possible to doubt the truth of these warnings?

QUESTIONS AND ANSWERS

Question: Can you at this stage say anything about the statement, "I and my father are one"?

J.G. Bennett: It means that Christ was aware that he was entirely open, that no barrier existed between him and the Higher Consciousness.

Q.: If only those who have paid the debt of their existence can feed the hungry, does it follow that those who not having paid the debt of their existence do not feed the hungry only increase the suffering of the Creator?

J.G.B.: Yes. If you will read the passage* from which I quoted [at the start of this chapter], it says almost word for word what you have just said. If we can really begin to see that, then we know that time is counted against us.

You understand, when I speak about feeding the hungry, there is more than one meaning to such a saying. There is one feeding of the hungry that belongs to the first stage, that is, the universal moral obligation to help our neighbor. There is the feeding the hungry that belongs to the second stage; there is in each of us a certain task to be accomplished in life and that task has no meaning unless it is for the good of our neighbor and especially for the food of future times. That is, in another and a very much higher sense, a feeding of the hungry that concerns the soul, and this is quite different again.

Q.: Is it not right to say that Christ is the Way?

J.G.B.: Quite right, but if you say it, then you must follow his way.

Q.: Wherein then lies the value of our mistakes?

J.G.B.: Mistakes have to come. Always, everywhere, and in everything there are mistakes. No finite being is so perfect that he is exempt from mistakes. They are part of the whole structure of the world. Mistakes are the price that has to be paid for such a world as ours, and since mistakes are necessary, they must also be useful. Mistakes are part of what Gurdjieff calls, in another of his writings, "the ever-present reminding factor."

Q.: If I have understood your talks correctly, I take it that the main function of a human being is to be able to produce energy of a type that can be acceptable to higher beings and also be of value to him in his later life. Can you tell us what is the nature of this energy? How would I be able to recognize it? Is it in thought power or is it something that we know in a different form? And how is it transferred from human beings to higher beings?

All and Everything, p. 386

J.G.B.: You said the main function. I would say the primary function. There is beyond that primary transformation not one but a whole range of possible destinies open to man, according to what he can accomplish. If we speak about the primary task as being the transformation of energy, I would say that it is the Energy of Consciousness. If I could be sure that you and I mean the same thing when we say thought power, I might say yes to that also. Or we can put it another way, if the word energy of consciousness seems strange, I can say that it is the energy of experiencing. Only nearly all our experience is wasted. That is to say, it just flows through automatic channels without building up any head behind it.

You remember that I spoke before about the difference between energy of fact and energy of possibility, or kinetic energy and potential energy. We can say that what is required of us is that some of the energy that is potential in our existence should be transferred into the general reservoir of potential energy. How is it transferred? It is transferred as it is set free, by every moment of separation. If there is a moment of separation in myself, when I divide affirmation from denial, something is liberated by that. One great separation occurs at the moment of death, and if I have not completed what has to be done by then, then it is at that moment, or in connection with that moment, that the transfer is completed.

Q.: You mentioned the significance of the number ten. Immediately, the teaching of [the Russian traveler and theosophist Helena Petrovna Blavatsky springs to my mind. Are the teachings of Blavatsky and Gurdjieff really about the same basic truths or are they both derived from something else?

J.G.B.: The use of the number ten to express totality is very ancient symbolism. It is not only an Eastern but also a Jewish symbolism and, therefore, would certainly be known to the compilers of the First Gospel. If you ask me about Blavatsky's teaching, I would say quite sincerely that there is very little teaching, very little significant content, even, in her big books. But some there is, and such is the extraordinary power of significant teaching that a grain of it can make a book different. Most books have not even a grain; maybe Blavatsky was given a grain because at that time it was needed.

Q.: You mentioned this evening both the Q'uran and the Gospels. Is Gurdjieff's system based on one religion in particular or what he considered to be the best of several?

J.G.B.: I quoted from the Q'uran and from the Gospels for convenience of elucidation. There is not one best. Where there is authentic teaching, it *is* authentic. It does not come from ordinary man. One thing is sure—that when ordinary men, with their ordinary capacities, try to build something up by taking a bit here and a bit there, from different teachings, they only make a hodgepodge. Several syncretistic hodgepodges have been produced in the last hundred years, but one cannot speak about Gurdjieff's Teaching as a syncretism taken from a bit here and a bit there. When you come to study it deeply, you can see that it springs from a new source.

Q.: "No man cometh to the Father except by me." Would you comment on that?

J.G.B.: I said this evening that the "I" can be understood as manifesting with different gradations as man himself is changed. I must, however, tell you this; I am not prepared to speak about anything connected with the Fourth Gospel.*

Q.: In the last of the three parables you repeated to us, you spoke of the separating of the sheep from the goats and said it was the separating of the affirming principle from the denying principle in us and that the denying principle had to go into the punishment of eternity. Can you tell us some more about what that means?

J.G.B.: There is someone in us that hides.** From this "someone that hides," various impulses enter our life, enter our experience, our consciousness, and so on. Unnoticingly, we identify ourselves with those; but then sometimes we see, really with dismay or even with horror, that there is present in us some attitude toward other people, toward our responsibilities, that we cannot accept, that we wish to repudiate. On the whole, we succeed in putting this aside and not letting it disturb us, but there remains that someone in us that wishes to hide.

To oblige ourselves to see that is a very painful thing. It does not mean that I suffer but that someone who wishes to hide cannot bear to find himself in the light. To be able to see ourselves so that someone remains under our eye, remains under observation, that is the punishment of eternity. It is one thing if we have not altogether betrayed the reason for our existence or entirely misused the talents that are in our hands—that is bad enough—but picture to yourself someone who has, and who has always refused to see that he has, but one day finds that he *has* to see it—who has refused to see it and finds himself compelled to see it.

Q.: You spoke of Blavatsky's teaching as a hodgepodge. What are your views on traditional teaching and religions of the past and the present and the process that has been going on for all these thousands of years? Would you also say that, in contradistinction to Blavatsky's teaching, that Gurdjieff's Teaching was really inspired by God or a Revelation perhaps?

J.G.B.: To have the possibility of seeing into reality is not so very rare. I spoke about it before. There is a part of all of us that is able to see that. With most people, it is always asleep. With a few, it wakes up. Sometimes it can wake up very strongly. People, then seeing things as they are, may make the mistake of thinking that what they have seen is all that has to be seen, and they proceed to interpret and build upon that, making use of various words and formulas they have learned from books. That does not mean that there was not a real seeing—if you like, a real revelation or a real inspiration. I thought suddenly of the Tai Ping movement in China a hundred years ago. Hung Hsiu Ch'uan saw something unquestionably; nobody reading of his experiences can doubt the reality of his visions. But when one studies what he taught on the basis of it, you see that

---

* The quotation is from John 14.6.
** (c.f. the Q'uran, chapter 114. "The people say I seek refuge with the Master of the people, the Lord of the people, the Obeyed One of the people, from the evil of the whisperings of him that hides, that whispers in the breasts of men." This chapter also gives the three stages of the manifestation of "I" as Master [Rabb], Lord [Malik] and the Obeyed One [Ilah]. It is the last chapter of the Q'uran.

he rushed at once from some vision of things as they really are into making use of what he had read about Christianity, about Taoism, about Communism, and so on. To be able not to do that, that is the mark of a great man. I say Gurdjieff was a great man because, having seen, he went on looking and never was satisfied until the end of his life. Nor did he ever set himself up for one who had reached finality. People with revelations are rare but not very rare. Humble people are rare; but people who see something and remain humble are very, very rare.

Q.: What happens to the person who constantly sees his faults before him? Is he able to get out of the situation?

J.G.B.: To see before one is ready to see is very dangerous. It is possible to go mad from that. That is why there is order. For example, I spoke about the teaching of Buddha. If you take such a text, as from the *Digha Nikaya*, the "Fruits of the Life of a Bikku," it is a compendious statement of the way as it is understood by that line of Buddhist teaching. First, it is insisted on that it is necessary to adhere to the silas or canons of morality and follow that way until some inner strength has been established. Then it is necessary to be able to be free from certain harmful impulses—wavering, uncertainty, fear, and so on. Then only it is possible to begin to open oneself to see things as they really are—that is the four *jhanas*. If you study, for example, that one *sutra*, you will see, I think, a very remarkable parallelism, even in its construction, to the chapter of the Gospel that I have been talking about today. Always, in every wise teaching, it is taught that people must be able first to have something in themselves and then to look and see. There are ways by which people can be made to see before they are ready. They are terribly dangerous ways. When, however, a man has the strength to see, then that is the most necessary thing for him. When he sees, then his seeing alone is the way out of the situation. If he sees, sheep remain sheep, goats remain goats, and there is no confusion. Until he sees, he cannot tell them apart. You must know that this is one strange feature of our human situation: We do not know our own sheep from our own goats. Many little creatures that we treat as pet lambs are really the worst kind of goats.

Q.: I am still confused about the conflict between "yes" and "no." Yes, I will have a cigarette. No, I will not have a cigarette.

J.G.B.: You remember I spoke about engagement. Something must be engaged. "Yes, I will" or "No, I will not have a cigarette" may be something, but it may be nothing. For one man in one situation, it may be a genuine struggle; for that man, it is necessary, in order to pay his debts, that he should not smoke—but he will suffer if he gives up smoking. That is one thing. Another man is indifferent. For yet another the decision is all illusory—he thinks that he says "yes" or "no" but he does nothing of the kind. He thinks that he decides whether to smoke or not, and what he does simply happens.

I will tell you one little story about one early meeting when we were studying these ideas with P.D. Ouspensky. It must be thirty years ago or more, in 1922. We were trying to find out about the struggle of "yes" and "no," and all of us decided to take some habit and say "no" to that habit and to come back the following week to our group meeting and report what we had found. One man reported that he had been sitting in the underground train coming to the meeting that evening and was thinking to himself, "This does not really teach one anything about the struggle of yes and no because there I was—I decided to give up smoking and did so, and it has not even been a struggle." As he was thinking that to himself, he looked and saw that he had a lighted cigarette between his fingers. The moral of which is: The struggle of "yes" and "no" does not exist in sleep.

Q.: Am I right in assuming that some people do not have a talent at all given to them? If that is so, what happens to them?

J.G.B.: No. Everyone has. Everyone has the pattern of his own possibilities, even the very weakest. The meaning of the parable is that some cannot do anything alone.

Q.: Does that mean that schoolwork is the only way for most people and for the other people that they can carry on on their own? They can work entirely on their own?

J.G.B.: No, neither the one nor the other can work alone. The difference is only in the amount of force that each has. Some have such force that their work can also sustain the work of others, whereas these others have not enough force unless they can share. It certainly does not mean that those who have force are able to work alone because it is an essential part of the work that they should sustain the force of others; therefore, the schoolwork is as indispensable for them as it is for the others. Moreover, you should understand also that no matter what force we may have, none of us can find the way alone. We all need a teacher.

About the other part of your question: "Does everyone need a school?" That is true only if you interpret the word "school" in a very wide sense. What we have to realize, though—I must say this otherwise I will not be giving the right impression—is that here we speak about the normal organization of human existence.* Our life is abnormal. Normal existence for man would be such that the strong helped the weak and the weak shared their possibilities with the strong. Our life is not like that at all; on the contrary, the strong exploit the weak and the weak drain the energy of the strong. Neither acts toward the other as he should. It is hard to say which is worse, those who have possibility of work and use their strength only for their own egos or those who are passive and merely wish to be supported without giving anything in return.

Q.: If one has enough force to sustain the work of others, and knows the way in which one could do so, and they do not want one to do so, how can that force that one has be effective if others do not recognize that one can help?

J.G.B.: If one can, people will recognize it, but nobody can. Who can? Can you? Can I? We cannot.

Q.: Not sustain, perhaps, that is going too far. We can help by our force.

J.G.B.: How? What do we know or *understand* about people's needs?

---

* c.f. the chapter in *All and Everything* entitled "The Organization for Man's Existence Created by the Very Saintly Ashiata Shiemash," p. 366. The word "normal" must not be confused with "usual" or "ordinary"—"normal" means as it should be according to true standards.

Q.: I was assuming that people did have a vision of the knowledge of another person.

J.G.B.: What is the use of assuming something that is not so?

Q.: Are there not some without talents? I was thinking of the mentally deranged—and I go from anything, from the extreme to moderate individuals. They are not free. Can they be described as being without talents? Or what is their situation?

J.G.B.: They can be described as spoiled people, people who, for a reason perhaps not of their own fault at all, cannot do what is required of them. Such situations do certainly arise by reason of our abnormal conditions of existence, and much more than they should. Too many people are born with a heredity—or with early conditions of life—that is a stumbling block to them or some shock prevents them. It is so.

Q.: Why does life appear to give such heavy odds against some people? Is it that their possibilities are equal to taking very severe strain or is it quite unconnected?

J.G.B.: You remember someone asked about mistakes and I said mistakes are everywhere. We cannot suppose that the world is ordered so that everything fits just as it should fit. It is not so. We do not live in that kind of world. It does not always mean that if someone has the odds heavily loaded against them that they have some corresponding strength that enables them to overcome that.

We have to see that the world is as it is. What I have spoken about this evening is how to interpret the phrase "the debt of our existence." It has to be acknowledged that some people without fault of their own are unable to pay this. It may be the fault of their parents; it may be something that has nothing to do with them. The present is what it is, but it may be possible to change the future. We can only reap now the harvest sown in the past, and if we feel compassion for the sufferings of the present and we wish a different harvest for those that are to come, we must sow different seeds now. If you read and study Gurdjieff's book, *All and Everything,* you will see that all the way through he teaches this idea, that is, to do in the present something for the future.

Q.: Must we regard these spoiled individuals as being in some sense irredeemable, and are they lost forever?

J.G.B.: But who are they? Who is lost?

Q.: You say the mentally deranged are spoiled individuals. Are they lost?

J.G.B.: I say who are they? Who is lost? Is a body lost? If there is nothing but a body—we know what happens to bodies. When you say they, about whom or what do you speak? If there is something in them that is able to live, then that something has a problem in front of it. If there is not, then there is no problem.

Q.: Then it never hurts, does it? Because if you die only automatic centers die, you are not conscious of being anything, and therefore the punishment does not exist. So what does it matter? If you think it does matter, then it stems through fear really?

J.G.B.: That is right. If it is so; that means that if there has not been a rejection of possibilities, as I said several times this evening, that is not the serious matter. What is serious is to have possibilities and not to use them; to be able to serve and not to serve; to be able to help and not to help but even hinder. That is the situation that Gurdjieff calls a situation of *hasnamuss*. But not someone who has not the possibility. He is not called into account for that. In the parable of the talents, it is very clearly said that the servant knew the situation and failed to do what was open to him to do, that is, to go and join others who were stronger than himself.

Q.: Then when he dies a physical death, he has some sort of consciousness that suffers?

J.G.B.: That is my next lecture—about death [*See* chapter 6]. I will speak about that then.

Q.: However humbly one may venture to do it, true service is being able to help other people. I think most people have experienced a kind of inspiration. They have not thought it out for themselves. It comes.

J.G.B.: You remember I said that there are different gradations of service. There is the ordinary moral sense that requires that we should do what we can in front of somebody's trouble. But also you must understand that we do not know what to do. Can we tell, in fact, whether the true essential welfare of a person is advanced by giving them bread or by withholding it from them? We must really know something to be able to judge that. Can you judge?

Q.: I think sometimes one is directed that way.

J.G.B.: Maybe one thinks one is. One must be very cautious about believing such "intuitions." That is what I say. People may, and do, have impulses coming from a higher part in themselves or a higher place or a higher consciousness. It is only very wise people who learn not to take these things without testing and studying and learning. As we know from history, people who believe in their own inspirations always come to something bad, even when they believe their inspirations are for good. No. One must know that, until a man is awake and can see, he cannot really trust anything because what is an inspiration from a higher level at one minute may, in another, perfectly well come in just the same form from his denying principle, and he will not know which is which. He really will not know.

I say the primary struggle of yes and no is based on what is in front of all of us, not on our inner inspirations. Trusting inspirations is a very dangerous thing, and all the more dangerous because sometimes they are authentic.

Q.: I was thinking of the people who had greater force, who had enough to sustain the work of others who had not enough force. Are not they to help the weak if they have a greater force?

J.G.B.: But force alone is not enough. I was allowing for that.

Q.: Can illusion enter into conscience?

J.G.B.: No, it cannot enter into conscience. But until a man is awake, he cannot know whether what appears to be conscience is indeed conscience or not.

"Only there, at the end of a certain time, does the principal and final sacred Rascooarno (death) occur to this two-natured arising after which such a 'higher being-part' indeed becomes an independent individual with its own individual Reason."

—*All and Everything*

Chapter 6

The First and the Second Death of Man

Lecture 6: April 12, 1954

PEOPLE NOWADAYS are accustomed to taking a rather lighthearted view of death. They believe, or say they believe, either that death is the end of our existence and, therefore, there is no reason to be troubled about what is beyond it or else they believe that they will continue to exist in some more or less pleasant and interesting way. In either case, they are, on the whole, untroubled. It is one characteristic of our present time that people find themselves able to put aside questions of this sort, either as if there were no answer and it did not matter or else as if the answer were rather easy and comforting. Such people, when they come to read the last chapter of Gurdjieff's book, from which I have quoted several times in these lectures,* and when reading what he says about the terror of death, they tend to mock at this and say that he exaggerates, that they do not feel any such terror.

Maybe they do not. Maybe they do not face the situation that exists rather deeper inside themselves. The truth is that many exaggerated things have been said about what happens to man after death, and, perhaps partly as a reaction from these exaggerations, people have come to minimize its importance or, at any rate, not to think very much about it.

Sometimes it is said that in eastern countries death is taken far less seriously than in the West, and that Eastern people have little regard for human life. This is far from being the case. Eastern peoples take death seriously. It is life they do not take so seriously. Last autumn, I went for a journey through some of the countries of southwest Asia—Moslem countries chiefly—and I met a number of interesting people, principally Dervishes. One man, among others interested me very much. He was the *bey* or head of a community of Dervishes greatly respected in southwest Asia, and I had many conversations with him. I can say that he is a saintly man of very unusual qualities. I refer to him because he told me the story of his life and of what first brought him into Dervish ways, because two of these stories are relevant to what I want to say about death, I am going to read you the notes that I made at the time, the same evening after I had talked with him.

---

* *All and Everything,* "From the Author," pp. 1219-38

At the age of seventeen, he was sent by his father to the Turkish military school in Istanbul, from which he passed with honors and became a gendarme officer. He fought in the Balkan wars but was never wounded. While still a young officer, an incident occurred that changed the whole course of his life. Two of his soldiers reported that they had been assaulted by a civilian, and one had been wounded. In time of mobilization, such a crime was punishable by death. He had the man arrested. He was court-martialed and condemned to death. After the verdict was announced, a deputation from the town came and begged for the life of this man, who was, they said, a great benefactor of the city. The bey sent the petition to the higher command, and, in due course, the man was reprieved and soon after released from prison. After the release, the bey was invited to meet the former prisoner and learned that he was enormously rich, owning great properties that he had inherited from his father, whose only son he was. They became friends, and the bey often visited his house, where he lived in the greatest luxury. Islam allows four wives, but this man used to marry girls of thirteen or fourteen, and when they reached fifteen or sixteen, he divorced them and took others. No *padishah* [a chief ruler] could live in greater luxury, for he had none of the anxieties of power and all the advantages of wealth.

So it continued for one or two years when the bey suddenly received news that his friend had died. He had been walking in his garden when he had reached up to pluck a ripe cherry from a tree and had felt a pain in his heart; and one or two hours later he had died. The bey was present for his burial.

The next day, the police received an anonymous communication saying that he had been poisoned by one of his wives, whom he was threatening to divorce; a postmortem was ordered. As he had no male relatives, the bey was asked to witness the exhumation on behalf of the family. When the grave was opened, there came the most abominable stench from the corpse and the bey almost fainted on seeing it. The face was distorted out of recognition, the abdomen and legs swollen, the skin black and blotched, and, worst of all, his body was covered with white maggots. This experience made a terrible impression on the bey. He had seen death on the battlefield, but he had never seen a corpse decompose so rapidly or so horribly.

As a result of this experience, he had turned his thoughts to the meaning of life and death. He began to study but could find no assurance. He could not accept the routine explanations given by the Hodjas and Ulema whom he interrogated.

Then, two years later, a second event occurred. One of his gendarmes had come to him in a state of great excitement and said that a man had died and that they wanted to bury him on top of his father, but when they opened the grave they found something so incredible that they wanted his advice. He went to the graveyard and saw to his astonishment that the corpse was perfectly preserved. He learned that the man had died forty-seven years previously. He was so amazed by this that he himself climbed into the grave and examined the body with his own hands. The skin was still soft and the body unblemished. When he smelled his hands, he perceived the most delightful odor. He took pains to verify beyond any doubt that this was indeed the body of the man who had died forty-seven years previously. Then the son was buried beside him and the grave closed.

This time, the bey was overwhelmed. He decided first of all to find out all that he could about this man's life. He established that he had been a man of no great worldly importance but had been noted for his uprightness and generosity. It was remembered of him that he had never harmed any person or any animal in his life.

Here were two facts that he had witnessed with his own eyes and had verified with his own senses. They could not be doubted, and yet they were inexplicable. Nothing in the religious teaching of Islam could account for such strange occurrences nor did they make sense according to the scientific and medical ideas that he had learned. He decided to search for an explanation. For one and a half years, he found nothing. Then he was advised by someone to seek out a certain dervish bey called Emin Keftarou. When he found him and told him the story, the Dervish listened very attentively. When the bey had finished, the dervish said, "If you have a room, and always keep it closed and dark, how will it become after a time?"

"Dank and smelly."

"But if you open the room to the air and the sun?"

"It will keep sweet."

"So it is," replied the dervish, "with the human body. It is like a room in which we live. It does not open to the visible suns but to the sun of God. So we must learn to give air and sun to this room in which we live. The first man kept his inner room in darkness, so it became foul and stinking. He was given by God great gifts that he should have shared with those who needed them. He did not do this, but he did worse. He lived only for the satisfaction of his body and thereby closed it to the air and light that come from God. His spirit, *nefis*,* lived in darkness, therefore when he died, his spirit could not free itself from his body until it was destroyed in the horrible way you describe. But with the second man it was quite otherwise. His spirit had turned toward God and left his body without difficulty. His body had been in his lifetime filled with air and light, therefore it remained clean, and being clean it did not decompose."

The bey said to the dervish Keftarou, "For one and a half years only one thought obsesses me, how to die like the second man and not like the first. Can you teach me this?"

Language differs. The words used in the account I have just read are perhaps different from the words that we should use, but we have to recognize the underlying truth, that is, that there are different ways of dying. These stories describe two extreme cases, but the difference in the two situations is a real one. All through these talks that I have been having with you, one thread has run, and that is the idea that man may accept or not accept the obligation to make a return for his existence. Last week, I spoke of the parable of the wise and foolish

---

*The *nefis,* in dervish terminology, is the consciousness of man, as distinct from his functions or his will.

virgins [*see* Chapter 5], and I said that this applies to all of us. We must understand that, in one important interpretation of this parable, it refers to the
moment of death and the difference between those who are ready for it and
those who are not ready. The preparation for death consists in making a separation in ourselves between that which has to perish and that which can have a different kind of existence—one that belongs to the world of our possibilities. We
can make this separation either intentionally now, during our lives, or involuntarily and helplessly at the time of our death.

There is a saying of Muhammed that when I first heard it made a strong
impression on me: "Die before you are dead." *"Mutu gablen temutu."* The same
thing has been said in many different forms. It means that we should separate
voluntarily that in us which can exist independently from that which must perish
before it is too late, for you may otherwise find that the separation has been
made without your knowing it and you have been left on the wrong side—that
is, really dead.

In its first and simplest interpretation, this saying of "Die before you are
dead" refers to the choice of "yes" and "no" that constantly returns to us and
puts us in touch with our own possibilities and our responsibility for the way we
use them. In the second lecture [*see* Chapter 2], you may remember that I spoke
about the four parts of man: the first three people in each one of us—the physical or bodily man, the emotional man, and the intellectual man—and the
absence of that harmonious working of these three parts in us that alone makes
it possible for the fourth part, the "I," to be present in us. Therefore, the first
part of our preparation for death must consist in bringing a harmony into our
functional life, in learning how to think and feel and see and hear and touch as
one person and not as a number of conflicting, unconnected centers of experience, such as all people we know are. Until we can come to some such balanced
experience, we cannot make that first separation by which our consciousness is
able to exist, to hold itself apart from the activity of our functions and from all
that is going on in our different centers. There is much work, much to be
learned, much that needs to be learned in achieving such a harmony of our functions. Under our present conditions of existence, they are disharmonized, and
thus even if we wish to do so, we cannot start by making that separation that
holds our consciousness independent of our functions—our "I" apart from our
centers. To go into that in detail would take us too far away from the theme of
our talk tonight. Only you must remember that if I speak about the preparation
for death, I refer first of all to this process of harmonization that must continue
throughout our lives.

Now let us speak about what we call death. We have spoken before about
the soul that is supposed to exist in man, and I must say again that we have to
see for ourselves how much confusion has entered all human thinking through
assuming that if there is a soul in man, it must be present in everyone and that it
must have certain properties—such as immortality and the possibility of existing
independently of this body of ours. If we believe in an immortal soul, and suppose that we have only this life in which to do anything to prepare for the future,

then our actions in this present life are decisive, and we are drawn into the doctrines of everlasting salvation and everlasting damnation, which have so disastrously diverted people's attention from their real problem. However, if we think more plausibly that a soul always exists in man, and is born over and over again and, in that way, we appear to have overcome many of the awkward questions that surround the idea of an immortal soul that has only one chance, then we also deceive ourselves, for if I speak of "I" or myself, I must mean someone who remembers. Without memory, who or what could "I" be? Because we can remember only this life, we really have no justification at all for supposing that anything exists that could pass from one life to another. The more we study and the more carefully we examine ourselves, the more we are bound to be convinced that no such thing does exist in man. If we had a soul, it would be the same from one year to another, from one day to another, from one minute to another; but when we observe ourselves, look at our experience, at our behavior, and look also at the behavior of other people, we see that one thing is certain, and that is that no one is always the same. No one remembers all that has happened to them, and even such memories as we do have are broken up into different lines or threads, quite unconnected with one another. So altogether we find a situation that cannot be reconciled with any belief that there is a soul in man. I repeat this because ordinarily we think that the question "Has man something that survives death?" can be answered by a simple yes or no. Either "Yes, he has a soul that lives forever" or "No, he has no soul and disappears with the death of the body." This tendency of ours to think in terms of absolutes leads us into all kinds of foolishness. It is one of the healthy signs of our present time that we are beginning to get away from this absolute kind of thinking.

The truth is that "something" does continue to exist after the death of the body, but it is very different from what we ordinarily would describe as an immortal soul. You remember I spoke about dreams and said that we live in an odd way, half in dreams and half in the unconscious activity of our organism. There very seldom is any interaction between what is really going on in our bodies, in our feelings, and so on and what we call our "thoughts" but are really our "dreams." Our dreams have a certain possibility of existence that is not altogether dependent upon what is happening in the body, and so dreams can continue without the body. It is therefore important for us to study how this dreaming process works in us. For this, we must come back to *attention* and see what attention really is. You remember that I described it as that form of energy that stands between Possibility and Fact. It is at any given moment the point of contact between our possibilities and our facts. It is a frontier that joins the two worlds. This means that it is energy of a higher quality than the energy by which our bodily organism works. Because of that, it has a force that our ordinary bodily energies do not have.

Now I am going to give you another picture of attention that may help you to see the part that it plays in connecting together the different threads of our life. You can compare attention to a belt conveyor; it is a piece of equipment installed in factories in order to transfer the material on which the factory is working from one department to another. Whatever is put on that belt conveyor travels with it to the next department. Our attention is like that. It has a carrying power: that which is put on it goes forward to another part of our experience, either from one of our centers to another center or from this moment to another moment. It is quite indifferent to what is put onto it; as with a belt conveyor, you may put on the material that the factory really needs or else you may put on any kind of rubbish and so load up the conveyor that there is no room for the goods and articles with which the factory really should be working. If we picture to ourselves a factory with a lot of careless, undisciplined workers who throw anything that they feel inclined to onto the belt conveyor and thus disorganize the whole work of the factory, we can have a good picture of our own life, where we allow anything to load up our attention, irrespective of whether what goes onto our attention has any importance for the real significance of our existence, for the transformation of energy that it is our obligation to transform.

Some of you were together yesterday when I made, with quite a number of people, an experiment to show how this carrying power of attention can be studied, and to see how involuntarily that which is put onto our attention is carried forward and reappears again at other stages—just like something that is put onto a conveyor and that reappears at different points in the factory until someone takes it off. The point about such an experiment is that once the object is loaded onto the conveyor or the experience is placed onto the attention, it goes forward automatically. For this, it is only necessary that the attention should be charged with the idea with sufficient power and emphasis or that it should be charged sufficiently frequently. With us, our experiences, very strong experiences, or experiences that are repeated over and over again get onto our attention in this way and are carried forward. Now this is the significant point for our subject tonight, namely, that this conveyor can go through the moment of death. Something is carried forward onto our attention, past death, and reappears on the other side. It reappears in the form of dreams.

We know from experience that what occupies our attention is constantly being displaced by different shocks. If we have a very small shock, and our attention is strongly occupied with something, we scarcely notice it and continue experiencing what is already there, but a stronger shock will deflect the line of our experience and we will follow that. A very strong shock may break it all down for a time. An experience may stop and only be picked up again later on, after what we call a period of unconsciousness. The separation that comes at death between this part that continues and our ordinary mechanical functions is a very big shock. At death, all from that part of us that belongs only to the world of facts from that which has some connection with the world of possibilities is separated. It is separated exactly at that point through which our attention passes. But after the effect of the shock has worn off, the dreaming is resumed. Then very much depends upon the situation that has been prepared.

If, during life, a man has allowed his attention to be occupied automatically without resistance or without any important resistance, by whatever happens to attract or interest him at a given moment, then his dream state is completely automatic and involuntary and he has no control over it. Alternatively, if, during his life, he has struggled in relation to some definite distinction of values, to accept certain things, and to reject others that approach his attention, then he can acquire the power of controlling his dreams and so of controlling the situation in which he finds himself after death—but only if he has acquired that power during life. That is one most direct meaning of the parable of the wise and foolish virgins. You remember how in this parable all the virgins, without exception, have to produce the oil, but some produce it in time and are ready while others produce it too late and are left outside; that means that everyone has to go through the whole of the experiencing that is allotted to them, but with some it is possible to control this in such a way as to open fresh possibilities while with others it is not. Then these latter people have to continue in the situation of those unhappy virgins of the parable who are left outside with their lamps burning in the darkness, serving only to remind them of their own foolishness. If we think about it deeply, we must see that it cannot be otherwise than this; it is impossible that we should go through life wasting our opportunities and not have to reap the consequences.

The "something" that is produced in man as a result of his life and that continues afterward in the dreamstate has only a provisional existence. It is able to continue so long as the possibilities that were inherent are not used up—so long as the oil has not burned itself out. There is one other passage I wish to read to you tonight in this connection. It is from one of Gurdjieff's writings [*Meetings with Remarkable Men*], in which he describes a talk with his father about this question of the soul and death. He attached great importance to his father's experience and to his wisdom, and he says that at his last meeting with him, he put this question to his father, and asked what conclusions he had come to as a result of his life, which had been well spent.

"How shall I put it?" his father answered. "In that soul which, as people believe, a man supposedly has, and of which they say that it exists after death independently and transmigrates, I do not believe; and yet at the same time, during the life of a man, something does form itself in him. That is for me beyond all doubt. As I explain to myself, a man is born with a certain property, and, thanks to this property, certain of his experiences during his life elaborate a certain substance, and from this substance there is gradually formed in him something or other which acquires a life almost independent of the physical body. When the man dies, this something does not disintegrate together with the physical body, but only much later, after the separation from the physical body. Although this something is formed from the same substance as the physical body of a man, yet it has a much finer materiality and it must be assumed a much greater sensitivity towards all kinds of perceptions."

The energy of our consciousness is energy in potential form. It is not the actualized energy of our physical bodies; and it is this potential energy that is this finer materiality, with its much higher sensitivity than ordinary matter, that is spoken of in this passage. It has also a certain possibility of cohering, and, if a man works in a certain way, this finer energy forms in him something that is not only capable of an independent existence but also of independent action; that is to say, the man in whom has been established the "I" of which I spoke in the fourth lecture [see Chapter 4], can acquire, through this process of the transformation of energy, a vehicle for that "I." This vehicle is a second body, like our ordinary physical body but composed of energy in this finer state that is not subject to disintegration by the same forces as cause the disintegration of this physical body that we see and touch. The man who has formed in himself this second body and whose "I" is able therefore to function independently of the physical body stands, at the moment of separation of the bodies, in a situation altogether different from that of the man who has not formed it. That "something" of which Gurdjieff's father speaks, and which continues only as a dream for ordinary people, has with him the possibility of further conscious transformations.

Before I go on to speak about the second body, and to what it leads, I must make sure that you recognize that this state is not like our ordinary daydreams that proceed against the background of sense experiences and bodily activities. We do have daydreams all the time, but we have the means to separate from them because we are present here in this body, which enables us, as we say, to bring ourselves back to earth. However, the situation of this "something," when separated from the physical body, is that it has no such means of verification, and therefore its dreams appear to have, for it, all the qualities of our life of fact. We have to picture to ourselves what can be the situation of a being who is obliged to dream and yet has moments of realizing that he is no longer in a form of existence out of which something further can come. That is why so many of Christ's parables refer to "weeping and gnashing of teeth" as the state of someone who can do nothing about the situation in which he finds himself and either partly or altogether realizes it.

Nevertheless, all such situations come to an end in time because there is in any given being only a limited store of possibilities for conscious experience. This applies also to this second body, of which I spoke just now. The second body is formed consciously in man by the struggle of "yes" and "no" that brings about what Gurdjieff calls "crystallization." This body has only a certain period of existence and then also has to disintegrate, but being made of potential energy, the energy itself cannot perish but goes into new formations in different ways, and in this consists what is sometimes called "reincarnation." As I have already emphasized, such reincarnation is only the "reusing" of the fragments of crystallized consciousness that remain after the dissolution of the "something" that survives. The dissolution of the second body is what Gurdjieff calls the second or final Rascooarno or separation. What is it that is then liberated or set free?

To understand this, we must return for a moment to the division, made at the beginning of these lectures [see Chapter 2], of function, consciousness, and will and understand that this physical body of ours—with its thoughts, feelings, and sensations—belongs to the world of function. It is a fact that, like all facts, endures only for a time and then disappears forever, but consciousness is not a fact—it belongs to the world of possibilities—and our second body is a body of consciousness. This body does not disintegrate except through the exhaustion of its possibilities. The third body is utterly different from either of the first two. It is a body of will. It does not actualize and it is not even dependent upon possibilities. It is the pattern. It is the shape of what we are that is not born and does not die. Nevertheless, the situation of man in regard to will again depends entirely upon what he has prepared in life, because although the pattern is there, and the will itself comes from a different sphere altogether from that of either the functions or the consciousness of man, our relation to it depends upon what we become. It is possible for man, if he chooses, to prepare for himself something that, after the dissolution of the first two bodies, is able to be the vehicle of the will and that can then enter into a process of transformation that ends with the final perfecting of the individual and his reunion with the Source.

You will see now why so much confusion exists about the soul because people confuse the will, which is eternal, with the consciousness, which is persisting. They also confuse the second body, which is able to survive death, with the will, which stands outside of time altogether.

We have, each one of us, a certain pattern to our existence, a part that we can play in serving the needs of the Great Being to whom we belong. If we accept to serve, we have to struggle with something in us that denies and repudiates this debt. It is the struggle between that which decides to serve something greater than ourselves and that in us which wishes only to take for ourselves. It is the liberation from that egoism that is the second and deeper meaning of the saying "Die before you are dead" and that is referred to in the concluding passages of Gurdjieff's book, *All and Everything,* when he speaks of the death of the tyrant in us.* It is a different struggle from the first. The struggle of "yes" and "no" may proceed in man without a separation from his own egoism, and the formation of the second body may come from motives that are very mixed indeed; the corresponding consequences will then have to be faced. However, the arising in man of that which can truly be called the Immortal Soul comes from this final struggle, when he sees in himself that which is ready to surrender itself altogether to service to the higher and that in him which altogether repudiates this.

There is very much more to say about this, but I have wished in this last lecture to return to the title that I gave to the whole series, that is, "Man's Task and His Reward." Work must not be for a reward. Everything that is done for a reward returns into our own egoism. But if man will turn away from any desire for reward and give himself to this service, then he finds himself in the position of the servant, in the parable of the talents, who brings back what was entrusted to him together with that which he has gained besides. That gain is the body of his will, and he finds that these things are made his own and that he is able to be an Independent Individual in the cosmos.**

For each one of us there are different possibilities of these attainments. I have necessarily spoken this evening in terms of that which befalls an individual—a single person—as he passes through the different stages of separation, but we have to understand that, as we need one another in life, we need one

---

* *All and Everything,* p. 1232.
** *All and Everything,* p. 763-65.

another far more in death. To be alone in death is more serious than being alone in life. External relationships serve for nothing in death; it is only the inner relationships of the essence of man that are able to pass through this barrier.

I spoke also about the will, as if the act of will by which man decides to serve were something that concerns him alone, but you will understand from all that I have been saying in these lectures that it cannot be so. Everyone who takes a decision takes it not only for himself but for all of those with whom he shares a relationship of being. Very, very few are able to take such a decision on their own initiative, but through the sharing of many, there can be participation in a greater will than the will of any one separately. In this is our great hope. It is this that we must try to understand. At the same time, we must know that the work by which a man acquires something that is able to control itself after death cannot be done by another. It is of such a nature that each one of us must do that work for himself. If we do not prepare the power to control our own state in life, we shall not be able to control it in death. Then we shall find ourselves obliged to be the passive spectators of our own dissolution.

Maybe I have tried to cover too much ground this evening and too many gaps have been left in what I tried to say. There are many things that it would be easier to make clear by means of questions and answers, so I hope that you will speak about any of the things that I have obviously omitted for lack of time.

QUESTIONS AND ANSWERS

Question: You have shown in all these lectures the need for us to look into ourselves in order to integrate ourselves, to form the "I" and ultimately the second body that would be separated from our physical body at death. But all this struggle and this work seem to be, from what you have said, for the sole purpose of the preparation of death. I feel this is a very dangerous philosophy because people will be liable to be so concerned with saving themselves for the purpose of death that they will forget to live for this life, in order to live a fuller life and lead a life that will be more useful to the community. I am afraid that it might tend to make people very self-centered, and I would like to hear your views on that.

J.G. Bennett: I said that there is one means only by which the final separation can be prepared, and that is by service. Service is what we have to do here in this life in the world of facts. Not only do we have to serve the needs of those with whom we are in immediate contact but, above all, we have to serve the needs of the future. You know that I have said, over and over again, that Gurdjieff's work does not consist in withdrawing from life. It does not consist in repudiating any of the obligations of life. We have the obligation toward ourselves to live our own lives with their possibilities. We have obligations toward our immediate surroundings, our families, our dependents. If anyone thinks that he can carry out his own inner transformation by turning his back on the outer life, he deceives himself entirely, and he is in great danger of being quite lost in dreams. Our chief recourse against the danger of being lost in dreams is to learn how to live outwardly and how to fulfill the obligations of our outer life.

Q.: When you speak of obligations, do you just mean the obvious obligations when people ask you for help or do you go as far as seeking the need that is not obvious and helping there?

J.G.B.: But this is what I spoke about chiefly last week [*see* Chapter 5].

Q.: Yes, I know, but …

J.G.B.: I spoke about the different stages with which a man can come in contact with his obligations. There are obligations of function, there are obligations of consciousness, and there are obligations of will. We cannot jump over the first two in order to arrive straight at the last. You remember I quoted Gurdjieff's picture of the four rooms that man has and the temptation that some people have to try to break through directly into the fourth room. It is the room of the will, and how, if they have not prepared by going through all that is necessary in the other three, they may reach that fourth room, but find it only empty. It is so arranged that all obligations have to be fulfilled in all parts, and we are so made that there is something in us that can do each of these.

Q.: When we realize that we are in the prison house of the self, how can we seek to become free so that we may serve?

J.G.B.: The whole work is concerned with the answer to that question. It is about the most sensible question anyone could ask. I have not in these lectures spoken at all about the practical application of these ideas or about the methods of work that Gurdjieff taught us. Those of you who wish to learn about that can come to a series of lectures that I shall give later this summer [in 1954,]* when again I shall try to show some principles of this work, but I must say to you here and now that I cannot promise that opportunities for further work or further study will be available. It is not so easy to arrange, and it really can only be arranged for those who have a real feeling of need for it.

However, taking your question as you put it, I would say that, first of all, we may know in rather a general, vague way that we are in prison somehow; that we are not able to be ourselves. Our manifestations, our outward behavior never correspond to what we wish. We are never able to be true, even to what we understand, but what it is that intercepts our decision and turns it into a manifestation very different from what we intended, all that has to be learned. Then also we must learn how to struggle so that we can have something in us able to direct our functioning. Again, we have to learn what part of our functioning we can change and what part of it we have to accept because it is part of the necessity of our existence that it should be as it is. Learning these things enables us to go more directly toward the aim, and the better we understand what is involved, the straighter we can go. But the aim must always be the same, however it may be formulated; it must be to fulfill the task for which we are here.

Q.: You said once that one's work has an influence on the fate of one's parents. This seems to be a reward that goes further even than the one you outlined, and I wonder how it connects.

J.G.B.: No, it does not go further because we are not separate from our parents. It is not possible for me to pay the debt of my existence without at the

---

* Publisher's Note: To be the subject of another book, if there is interest. Please write.

same time paying my part of the debt of my parents. Therefore, the work that I do must be for my parents also, and the better I understand that and the more consciously I accept it, the closer I will come to discovering what I really am. I said that a man can finally become himself, and such a man is a source from whom possibilities radiate. The possibilities he creates enter into his parents also.

Q.: Does it follow then that if your parents have fallen far short of their obligations, that in doing that you will have to undertake far more?

J.G.B.: Yes, it is so. We do have to undertake far more than what is involved in the results just of our own life. But also we must understand that this is to our advantage. *To be able to pay* is the best possession man can have. All my experience over many, many years has proved this to me, that people who repudiate their parents sooner or later come to a standstill in this work. People who do not accept and love their parents are cut off from possibilities. I have heard Gurdjieff say that many times, and I myself have seen it with my own eyes in hundreds of cases, and now it is for me an established truth. Not to love one's parents is an almost insuperable handicap in the work.

Q.: Do you demand of children who have been cruelly treated by their parents that they should love them?

J.G.B.: Why not? What else should they do?

Q.: Oh, certainly not. Cases of people scalding their children that we read about, the mother scalding her child with boiling water. Do you demand that they should love their parents. Such parents are abnormal, and the child should be made to see that. I cannot see where the love comes in there at all.

J.G.B.: I can only repeat what I said. It is an observed fact that people who bear resentment against their parents for anything that has been done to them—and, of course, parents ill-treat children in many ways and even deprive them of possibilities—are themselves the ones who lose because something closes for them, and to encourage children to have resentment toward their parents is really a great sin.

Q.: What about abnormal parents?

J.G.B.: I speak here about a relationship that exists. You speak about abnormal parents; but we have to accept that, if there is some abnormality in our parents, we share in this. We cannot repudiate them on account of their abnormality. Something of it will have entered into us also, and we have to eradicate it in ourselves. We have to accept this as a task that applies to all of us. Nobody has been presented with a spotless heredity. Every one of us have weaknesses that we have inherited from parents and grandparents and so on. We have to accept this. By overcoming these weaknesses in ourselves, we liberate both past and future generations. In that way, we can break the line of transmission. But I think perhaps we have spoken enough about parents and should come to some other aspect of our problem.

Q.: Could I ask you to comment on the two following phrases? One, "I am the captain of my soul." Two, "Let us eat and drink; for tomorrow we shall die." Following from that, could you not, by indulgence, reach a stage of passivity when nothing has any interest to you, and therefore by negation you would reach a state of complete disinterest in this?

J.G.B.: Why should I comment on them? The first is nonsense. The second is stupidity.

Q.: That is a matter of opinion.

J.G.B.: You asked me to comment.

Q.: During the last war [World War II], I was always very concerned about all those young men who were cut off from life, seemingly through no fault of their own. Could you tell me if any special facilities exist for those people to enter the top story, or are they just wasted lives? I am very serious about that question.

J.G.B.: Do you think I am not serious about it? Nearly all of my best friends when I was at school were killed. I happened to be at just such an age that many of my schoolfellows were killed in World War I in 1914. We have to understand this—that the young man or the child that dies without his possibilities having been fulfilled is not called to account for them. The pattern of his will remains unspoiled and from it new actualizations can arise. It is quite a different situation for those of us who remain. Sometimes people say to me, "My child that died or my son who was killed, shall I see them again?" We must understand that this depends on us, not on them. We are in the serious situation, not they, because our possibilities are being used up all the time. We shall have to give an account for what we have done with what has been entrusted to us. If we are able to be in our own essence, then we can have an essence relationship. You remember I said in the lecture that to be alone after death is a most serious thing. In life, we are accustomed to outward relationships, relationships of function only. We must know that those external relationships cannot survive the dissolution of the functions. It is only the inner relationship of essence that survives. If we have not established something in us that is capable of an essence relationship, then it is we who are lacking, because those who die with their possibilities intact can form around those possibilities a new existence. However, those of us who die with our possibilities used up and wasted are not in that situation. We are accustomed to be sorry for those who die young. They are not the people to be sorry for. People to be sorry for are those who live out their lives and waste them. That is the most terrible, and the only terrible, thing. For a long time, I must tell you, I could not bear to think of my schoolfriends who were killed. Then the moment came when I was able to see their situation and mine, and I never since had any sorrow for them.

Q.: In attempting to achieve the aims you have spoken of in these lectures, has prayer any place, and, if so, would you say what form it should take, how it should be directed?

J.G.B.: Prayer consists in putting the right thing on the belt conveyor. That means, prayer consists in putting the right attitude into our attention. It must be done in such a way that it will remain there. If it is put on so weakly that the first impression will push it off again, such prayer has no meaning and no value. If prayer is experienced with the whole of our being, then it continues.

Moreover, prayer is a great means whereby people can share experience.

Prayer is relative to what man is. Man who is nothing, his prayer is nothing. If he is awake, his prayer is altogether different. Prayer is the acknowledgment of something higher, and it is the opening of ourselves toward something higher. That is one great part of the work of preparing in ourselves what should be there.

Q.: You have introduced for the first time in your talks the quality of love—loving one's parents, and so on. I take it that even if one knows and understands the doctrines, one would not go very far on the path unless one expressed his love as an expression of his possibilities.

J.G.B.: You know why I speak little about love? Because it is a word that we are not entitled to use about ourselves, about anything that we can experience. Our subjective states, that we like to call love, are never, never liberated from our own egoism. A man who is capable of nonegoistic, impartial love is already a man whose will is free. We are not such people. When I spoke about love of parents, it is the beginning of a right attitude. Even with all the faults that we have derived from our abnormal conditions of existence, it is really natural for man to love his parents and abnormal for him not to do so. To suggest that anyone should hate their parents, whatever they may be or whatever they may do, is falsification of everything that is real in human life.

Q.: Have you forgotten your promise to deal with the problem of the lower eating the higher? There are so many instances in nature of the lower consuming the higher rather than the higher consuming the lower because it is a problem that has kept many people away from the acceptance of any belief in a higher being.

J.G.B.: Yes, I had forgotten. You remember when you asked the question before, I said that there is a twofold movement, a movement up and a movement down—evolution and involution—and that both movements are necessary to the harmony of all existence. There is a separation always of the fine and the course, some that has to ascend and some that has to descend. Therefore, one part of the answer to your question is that that which is coarse descends, as the worms consume the body; but, of course, it is not the whole of the answer.

There is another and deeper question about waste. Can we say that everything is perfectly worked out so that everything goes to the place that it should go to? That the coarse goes inevitably to the place where coarse things are and the fine to where fine things are? On the whole, it is so; but existence itself is inseparable from uncertainty. Time is such that the actualization of one possibility must be at the expense of another. Actualization is like that, and why it should be so goes back to the final "Why?"—Why is such a universe in existence? But the world being as it is, there has to be uncertainty; nothing is infallible anywhere on any scale.

I must tell you that when I came to realize that, it was the greatest relief of my life because to try somehow to believe that everything was exactly right, and foreordained by an omniscient and omnipotent Creator, had proved too much for me. When I realized that it is not so, that everything is not exactly right and cannot be and therefore among other things there must be waste and frustration and failure, by the very fact that the universe exists, I became at peace over this. You remember I have spoken about need, about our task, about service. Service would mean nothing at all if everything were perfect anyhow—or if there were an almighty omniscient chess player, moving each piece exactly to the best advantage, then we should have no part to play except to be moved and should not even be able to consent or refuse to be moved when his hand picks us up. Reality is not like that. We are objectively needed. Our work is necessary because without it the uncertainties and hazards of the universe would get out of hand. At best, we can hope to be a very small source of order in the universe. All that mankind could achieve, even if it were able to work harmoniously together, would still be a very small factor in the whole working of the universe. Yet man's work is really needed. I say that because I think that your question has something of that behind it. If it were simply, "Why do the worms feed on the body?" it would be very easy to answer because it would simply be the coarse going to its own place, but the fact that you have returned to it means, I think, that you feel that there is the problem of waste, of the greater having to be sacrificed to the less—a sacrifice not only of the greater beings but even of the greater purposes sometimes. It is because we live in such a world that our existence does really matter. We have something to do that has to be done.

Q.: I am trying to find out what Gurdjieff has that Christianity has not got. You have been speaking, to some degree dogmatically—if I may say so with all respect to you personally—about death and the beyond. What authority have you for pronouncing these sorts of judgments? Is your authority the comparative consensus of religion, the general opinion of the great mystics and the master religious teachers?

J.G.B.: The way the world works shows us that laws are everywhere the same. What we find out about man proves to throw light on the universe. What we find out about the universe throws light upon our own human existence. We can further say that what we find out about life also teaches us about death. All that I have been saying about death is not something remote and beyond experience. These things happen to us here and now. We go through all these processes of separation, the voluntary and the involuntary condition, the state of man who dreams only and cannot control his dreams. All those are things that we can find here in this life.

In my opinion, what is of supreme importance in what Gurdjieff has taught is that it is not dogmatic but it shows the way by which we ourselves can find answers to our questions. If I have told you briefly of conclusions that I have come to myself, without showing you all the steps by which I came to them, it is simply that there would not, in any case, be time for that because it requires a whole lifetime of experience. But I could not have reached my conclusions by myself. I could not have found answers to my questions if I had not been shown the way to look and shown the means to verify and test what I found.

What I have said today about death does not go beyond what we can find and verify in our own experience if we are prepared to look for it. Because, really and truly, everything that we need to understand we can find here in this very life. There are very, very few who can look and find by themselves, but what one cannot do alone, people who are prepared to share can. If you ask me what is distinctive about Gurdjieff's Teaching, I would say that he shows people not only how to work for themselves but how to work together, which is a much more difficult thing than it looks—much more difficult. Because of that, we can hope to reach assurances that scarcely anyone could ever reach if left to himself or if he chose to try to look alone.

SUPPLEMENTARY QUESTIONS AND ANSWERS
THE GROSVENOR HOTEL, LONDON, APRIL, 12, 1954.

Question: I found your first lecture most inspiring [see Chapter 1]. It encouraged me to look for something by which man must pull himself up by his own shoestrings, but after that the rest seemed to me a great mixture of various religions and various philosophies. There was no clear-cut design. To one who has interested himself in philosophies and religions, and especially in international relations, humanitarian principles, you do really create the idea that nothing is wanted except to help other people—doing your best for them, loving your neighbor, and so on, was the essential point of this teaching. I find that those countries where they are doing their best toward that point by giving service to their own people are just those that everyone despises and hates. How does that balance this present philosophy? How can one do anything in a world where service in any shape or form is not considered at all? The best we can hope to do is to gain merit. Taking into consideration the chaos that exists at the present day—I am speaking now of the atomic age—it will take many, many years for the world to embrace this religion, and may it not then be too late?

J.G.B.: Whatever I might have said and wherever I might have started, I should have certainly used words that would have sounded familiar to people, and at once they would have connected with those words their own meanings. There is only one way out of that; that is to use words that no one has ever heard of before, as Gurdjieff does in *All and Everything*. You use the word "service," for example, as if it meant something that anyone can do for the benefit of others, whereas I spoke of it as the goal, the last thing of all that is attained when a man can *see* and when he can *do*. We have to begin by realizing that *we do not know what others need*. We do not even know the meaning of such phrases as "love thy neighbor as thyself." We have to start much further back than most people want to start. They all want to start at once by "doing" something, by "doing good to others." The chief reason why we are in this chaos is that everyone wants to "do" something without understanding what is needed, without understanding how to "do." In consequence words like "service" are discredited, and we must not blame people for being very skeptical about talk of "service to humanity" and "good to others" and so on, when we see what disasters come out of it all.

The starting point for this teaching, Gurdjieff's way, is the realization that we do not "understand" and cannot "do" anything; that we have got, therefore, to begin at the beginning and find out something for ourselves that we can be sure of.

In preliminary talks such as these, we have to cover all the ground and go on to talk about some things that belong to the end, and it happens inevitably when you talk about things that belong to the end that people will think that they apply to the beginning.

You say that Gurdjieff's Teaching is founded on service. One might better say exactly the opposite, it has service as its apex and not as it foundation. At its foundation, it has understanding what our situation really is. Anyone can see—we can scarcely help it—that our human situation has got somehow out of hand. We all of us realize that we are getting to know more and more about all kinds of techniques that enable us to produce unbelievable results but that we have not the slightest idea how to control ourselves, how to behave, how to use what we have got. Not the slightest! Everyone can see that the world of today demands tolerance of us all. No one has the slightest idea how to be tolerant. As you rightly say, nobody is tolerant. Everyone finds other people are wrong and that they themselves are right. Always, you and I and every one of us, we are all the same. That is what I mean when I say we have to begin much further back than people like to think. Then you ask the further question, "Well, what about time? Is there time for these new ideas to take root?" If you start stirring things up too much in a hold full of gunpowder, you will be likely to blow the ship up all the quicker. First of all, one must learn how to take out the fuses, to learn how to make the situation a little safer, perhaps even in very small ways, on the scale where we can do so. If you have understood that on a large scale there is literally nothing to be done at the present moment—or at any other given moment—then you have seen something, but that need not be at all a pessimistic realization. I can see that there is nothing to be done on a large scale, but I may see also that there is something to be done on a small scale, and in place of a superficial optimism, that hides a deep pessimism, I begin to have genuine hope about being able to do something.

All the way through, ever since I began studying these ideas, one thing I saw was that something could be done; never as much as people wanted to do, never as much as I myself wanted to do, but something could be done. Whenever I tried to do too much, in any direction, I only spoiled it, like everyone else has always done, but when I was contented to do as much as I could do, then I saw that it was really astonishing how the situation would change.

Q.: But in our private lives, we have to start to do something, do we not?

J.G.B.: There is just as much gunpowder in our private lives as in our public lives, and if we try to do too much too quickly, we shall blow things up there also.

Q.: Will you tell me something about those who are excluded from this work?

J.G.B.: Whom do you think is excluded? Whom do you think cannot work this way?

Q.: Myself.

J.G.B.: What is to stop you?

Q.: My own ignorance. It seems to me this work is very selective.

J.G.B.: In what way do you call it selective? I ask you again, what is to stop you? Can you see anything that is to stop you?

Q.: No. But I do feel it would be difficult to grasp it for millions of people, the way it is put. Do you see what I mean? It is not simple enough.

J.G.B.: I have seen people touched by these ideas, and able to follow them, who were lacking in almost every kind of advantage. People with no education at all, with very hard conditions of life—really a hard kind of factory work; working all day in a noisy factory under almost intolerable conditions. They come into this work really in despair. They are unable to get a position in this country and are living in desperately hard conditions, and yet they prove able to work, and so able that I wish that I could have such force for work as they have.

Another thing, about India. I know a man who came from a very small Indian village, living under very bad conditions but who had the wish to find something, and he did. He finally arrived at Oxford, and from Oxford he came to see me and began to study these ideas, and I am always in touch with him and I see no obstacle at all nor does he. I will tell you one other thing, that Gurdjieff's name is more respected in India than it is in England. His work and his books are taken as authoritative in a way they certainly are not here. To say that people are unable to work because of their conditions of life or the kind of education they have, or the sort of country they come from—it is not at all true. People cannot work only if something is spoiled in them. That is what is serious—if they are unable to recognize possibilities when they come to them. Those who can recognize possibilities will do so, wherever they come from and whatever their conditions.

To possess the right to the name of "man," one must be one.

—*All and Everything*

"We are dashing against each other like boats:
Our eyes are darkened, though we are in clear water."
—Jeláluddin Rumi, Mathnawi
Reynold A. Nicholson trans.

OUT OF PRINT

alphabetical by title • *most recent edition is shown*

An Introduction to Gurdjieff's Third Series, Sherborne: England: Coombe Springs Press, 1975, 34p.

Approaching Subud,[†] Dharma Book Co., 1962.

Awareness of Others,[†] Shantock Press.

Breath, Shantock Press. 4p.

Christian Mysticism and Subud, London: Hodder & Stoughton, 1961.

Concerning Subud,[†] London: Hodder & Stoughton, 1958. 186p.

Conscious Labor and Intentional Suffering,[†] Shantock Press.

*Creation,** Sherborne: Coombe Springs Press, 1978. 141p.

Creative Thinking, Charles Town: Claymont Communications, 1989.

Crisis in Human Affairs (The), New York: Hermitage House, 1951. 238p.

Dramatic Universe (The), vol. 1, The Foundations of Natural Philosophy, Claymont Comm., 1987.

Dramatic Universe (The), vol. 2,[º] The Foundations of Moral Philosophy, Claymont Comm., 1987.

Dramatic Universe (The), vol. 3,[º] Man and His Nature, Claymont Communications, 1987.

Dramatic Universe (The), vol. 4,[º] History, Charles Town: Claymont Communications, 1987.

Dramatic Universe, A Short Guide, Daglingworth: Coombe Springs, 1982, 75p., glossary by M. Kaminski.

*Existence,** Sherborne: Coombe Springs Press, 1977. 74p.

Fallen Leaves, 5 vols., Pennsylvania: Private, 1976-80.

*Food,*** Sherborne: Coombe Springs Press, 1977. 50p.

God and Creation,[†] Not issued, Sherborne: Coombe Springs Press.

Gurdjieff and the Buddhist Mind-Body, London: *The Middle Way,* 1950, pp.14-16., w/ Cyril Moore.

•*Gurdjieff Today,*** Sherborne, Coombe Springs Press, 1974. 47p. In print as an appendix in *Is There Life on Earth?* (Bennett Books, 1989).

Gurdjieff: An Unknown Teaching,[†] Unpublished: 1952. Four lectures at Carnegie Hall.

Gurdjieff: the Unknown Teacher,[†] Unpublished: 1949. 4p.

How We Do Things, Charles Town, Claymont Communications, 1989. 69p.

Intimations: Talks with J.G.B. at Beshara, New York: Weiser, 1975.

Journeys in Islamic Countries, 2 vols., Sherborne: Coombe Springs Press, 1977. 123p. & 173p.

Life and the Demiurge,[†] Not issued, Coombe Springs Press. Incorporated into *Creation*

Living in Two Worlds, Shantock Press. 8p.

Long Pilgrimage: Life & Teaching Shiva.Baba, California: Dawn Horse Press, 1983.

*Material Objects,*** Sherborne: Coombe Springs Press, 1977. 56p.

*Noticing,*** Sherborne, Coombe Springs Press: 1976. 48p.

Paths to Spiritual Understanding, Shantock Press.

Radiations and Emanations, Daglingworth: Coombe Springs Press, 198?. 13p.

Sacred Impulses, Shantock Press. 8p.

Sevenfold Work (The), Charles Town: Claymont Communications, 1979. 160p.

Spiritual Psychology (A)(revised), Lakemont, Georgia: CSA Press, 1974. 268p.

Sufi Spiritual Techniques, Daglingworth: Coombe Springs Press, 1982. 18p.

*The First Liberation,*** Sherborne: Coombe Springs Press, 1976. 35p.

•*The Image of God in Work,* Sherborne: Coombe Springs Press, 1976. 74p. In print as a chapter in *Sacred Influences* (Bennett Books, 1989)

The Thematic Technique. (Intro.), Sherborne: Coombe Springs Press, 1976. 8p.

Transformation, Charles Town: Claymont Communications, 1978. 198p.

Values: An Anthology for Seekers, Kingston-up'n Thames: Coombe Springs Press, 1963. 169p.

Witness: The Autobiography. of John G. Bennett, Charles Town: Claymont Communications., 1983.

[º] Some copies of The Dramatic Universe (vols. 2, 3, & 4) may still be available from the publisher.

•These publications are in print as parts of other books published by Bennett Books.

*Studies from the Dramatic Universe series.

**The Sherborne Theme Talks series.

[†] The Bennett Books Library is in need of a copy of these publications. Donations and/or photocopies appreciated.

IN PRINT
by publisher and year of publication

BY BENNETT BOOKS PUBLISHING

Masters of Wisdom ISBN 1-881408-01-9. (August, 1995). 272 pp., Paper, Indexed.

Making a Soul: Human Destiny and the Debt of Our Existence. ISBN 1-881408-00-0. 1995. 128 pp., Paper, Indexed.

Deeper Man Foreword and epilogue by A.G.E. Blake. ISBN 0-9621901-9-5. 1994. 224pp., Paper, Indexed.

Elementary Systematics: A Tool for Understanding Wholes, Foreword by David Seamon. ISBN 0-9621901-7-9. 1992. 128 pp., Paper.

Gurdjieff: Making a New World ISBN 0-9621901-6-0. 1992. 272 pp., Paper, 6x9, Sewn

What Are We Living For? Foreword by Mrs. A.L. Staveley. ISBN: 0-9621901-8-7. 1991. 128 pp., Paper, New Material: "Who is Gurdjieff?"

Hazard: The Risk of Realization. Foreword by A.G.E. Blake. ISBN: 0-9621901-5-2. 1991. 128 pp., Cloth & Paper, Indexed.

Needs of a New Age Community: Talks on Spiritual Community and Fourth Way Schools. ISBN 0-9621901-2-8. 1990. 128 pp., Paper.

Is There "Life" on Earth? An Introduction to Gurdjieff. ISBN 0-9621901-1-X. 1989. 128 pp., Paper, New Material: "Gurdjieff Today."

Sacred Influences: Spiritual Action in Human Life. SBN 0-9621901-0-1. 1989. 96 pp., Paper, New Material: "Image of God in Work."

BY CLAYMONT COMMUNICATIONS

Energies: Material, Vital, Cosmic ISBN 0-934254-28-1. 1989. 128 pp., Paper.

BY SAMUEL WEISER, INC.

Idiots in Paris Diaries of Elizabeth & J.G.B. in Paris with Gurdjieff, ISBN 0-87728-724-4. 1991. 60 pp., Paper

Sex ISBN 0-87728-533-0. 1991. 75 pp., Paper

Talks on Beelzebub's Tales ISBN 0-87728-680-9. 1988. 167 pp., Paper.

Enneagram Studies ISBN 0-87728-544-6. 1983. 144 pp., Paper.

Gurdjieff: A Very Great Enigma ISBN 0-87728-581-0. 1983. 96 pp., Paper.

The Way to be Free ISBN 0-87728-491-1. 1980. 200 pp., Paper.

The above books are available from most book dealers or the publishers. You can also order directly from Bennett Books. Please use the order form at the back of this book.

These bibliographies are current as of February, 1995. Bennett Books welcomes information that would update or correct these bibliographies. Please write.

Bennett Books Publications
by J.G. Bennett

in print

Sacred Influences: Spiritual Action in Human Life, 1989
Is There "Life" on Earth? An Introduction to Gurdjieff, 1989
Needs of a New Age Community, 1990
Hazard: The Risk of Realization, 1991
What Are We Living For?, 1991
Gurdjieff: Making a New World, 1992
Elementary Systematics, 1993
Deeper Man, 1994
Making a Soul, 1995

forthcoming

Masters of Wisdom, 1995
Witness, 1995

BENNETT BOOKS
P.O. Box 1553
Santa Fe, N.M. 87504

505 986-1428 phone/fax

Books that Support Spiritual Development

WRITE OR CALL FOR LATEST CATALOG.

Thank You for Purchasing This Book.

Use this page to order directly from Bennett Books and receive *free shipping* when your order is $35. or more.

All titles are by J.G. Bennett
quantity/title (paper, unless otherwise noted)

	Price	Extended
__Making a Soul	$13.00	_____
__Deeper Man	$18.00	_____
__Elementary Systematics	$13.00	_____
__Gurdjieff: Making a New World	$17.95	_____
__What Are We Living For?	$11.00	_____
__Hazard: The Risk of Realization	$11.00	_____
__Hazard: The Risk of Realization (cloth)	$22.00	_____
__Hazard (cloth and paper; save $4.00)	$29.00	_____
__Is There "Life" on Earth?	$9.50	_____
__Needs of a New Age Community	$11.00	_____
__Sacred Influences	$8.00	_____
__The Planetary Enneagram	$2.75	_____
__Enneagram Studies	$7.95	_____
__Gurdjieff: A Very Great Enigma	$5.95	_____
__Sex	$6.95	_____
__Talks on Beelzebub's Tales	$8.95	_____
__The Way To Be Free	$12.50	_____
__Idiots in Paris	$9.95	_____
__Energies	$11.95	_____
	Sub Total	_____

If subtotal is less than $35 add $6.00 shipping & handling _____

*Even if the subtotal is over $35 add $6.00 to subtotal
if you want the books sent UPS* _____

• UNLESS YOU ADD $6 FOR UPS BOOKS WILL BE SENT BOOKPOST.
• BENNETT BOOKS IS NOT RESPONSIBLE FOR BOOKS SENT BOOKPOST.

NM residents please add 6.25% sales tax_____

Total enclosed _____

Check or MO in $U.S. drawn on a U.S. bank only; payable to:
Bennett Books: P.O. Box 1553, Santa Fe, NM 87504

For information call 505 986-1428

Name _____

Address _____

City_____State_____ ZIP _____

Phone_____ Date _____

MS-95